****"If you liked *Mr. Roberts* or *The Caine Mutiny* you'll enjoy this book."

West Coast Review of Books

Art Fettig's
UNFIT FOR GLORY

The wildly funny adventures of G.I. M.A.S.H. survivors reconfirming their manhood.

Copyright © 1987 by Art Fettig
All rights reserved including the right of reproduction in whole or part of any form.

Published by

GROWTH UNLIMITED, INC.

Art Fettig, President • 31 East Avenue S • Battle Creek, Michigan 49017
Phone 616-965-2229 or 616-964-4821

Manufactured in the United States of America

Library of Congress Catalog Card Number 86-081726
Fettig, Art
Unfit for Glory

ISBN 0-916927-02-4

0 1 2 3 4 5 6 7 8 9 0

DEDICATION

This book is respectfully dedicated to all of the men and women who have ever served in the American Armed Forces.

It is a tribute to all who have tasted the pain and glory of battle, with special honor to the combat rifleman.

The author wishes to further dedicate this book to all who served their country during the Viet Nam War. These men and women did their country's bidding at a time when they were forced to fight not only the enemy overseas but also the forces of public opinion at home.

As I travel around America giving speeches I always take time to ask our Viet Nam veterans to stand up and I ask the audience to join me in applause as a means of welcoming them home. Far too often, following my talks, the veterans come up and thank me for the gesture confessing that mine was the first welcome they had as yet received.

One veteran in Ohio recently told me that when he got off the plane from Viet Nam in San Francisco he was wearing his uniform with his decorations, a Silver Star for Valor and a Purple Heart with a cluster for twice being wounded and nearly losing his life. He said, "The welcome home I received was when a fellow came up to me in the airport and spit in my face and called me a murderer."

In Indiana, another Viet Nam veteran came up after my talk and my tribute and confessed that he had trusted me and stood up with the other Viet Nam vets and that it was the first time since he'd come home that he had admitted to anyone that he had served in Viet Nam.

I had the honor of speaking in Washington D.C. at the time they unveiled that beautiful statue of our fighting men in Viet Nam. I saw the thousands of Viet Nam vets in their battle fatigues and they were wearing their medals and decorations and many were on crutches and in wheel chairs.

If you are an American Viet Nam veteran I salute you. If you are not then I challenge you to find a Viet Nam veteran today and say, "Welcome Home."

Unfit for Glory is Fiction.

None of the characters or events in this book are real. The author was a combat rifleman, he was wounded in Korea and he did attend a Personnel Management Class at Eta, Jima, Japan.

During his time in the U.S. Army, the author did encounter officers and enlisted men who were not quite as good and not quite as bad as the G.I.s depicted in this work. Mostly, this is a reminiscence of things that never were.

Art Fettig is the author of so many books that he has truthfully lost count. He has authored popular books on sales, public speaking, mentoring, personal growth and positive parenting. A successful, internationally known speaker, Fettig is known as "The Wizard of Pos" because of his robot named "Pos" who teaches all of the secrets of happiness and success in his popular Three Robots series of books and tapes of children.

Unfit For Glory is a story that has been sitting around in Fettig's mind since he first started writing seriously in 1960. The novel has gone through many, many years of rewriting and revision. When Fettig first submitted the novel to publishers they told him that the time was not right for a story about Korea. Since then, another author's book "M.A.S.H.," also about Korea, was published and became first a hit movie and then a long, long playing T.V. success.

After years of waiting Fettig finally decided that the time had come for his story to find real life in print. Fettig laughs when questioned about the novel. "It's just something I felt must be done. There is a saying that points out that the greatest tragedy that can come to anyone is for them to die with their song unsung. Well the characters in my book, although truly fictional, are real people to me and I believe that each of them is saying something very important. I just cannot let them sit around in my file cabinet any longer. I think they deserve to sing their song too and I only hope the reader will discover from this story that noone, but noone, is truly Unfit for Glory."

1

Going South

If you've ever seen the movie or T.V. show, or even read the book M.A.S.H., then you've probably witnessed how Hawkeye and his fellow surgeons and nurses, at the Mobile Army Surgical Hospital, worked miracles every day to save the lives of the wounded combat soldiers in Korea.

Some of these wounded G.I.s made remarkable recoveries at M.A.S.H. units and were quickly shipped back to their combat units. Others were sent to hospitals in South Korea further back from the fighting. Some were evacuated to hospitals in Japan for more surgery and convalescence and many more, with more severe injuries, were sent home to the United States for extensive hospitalization and eventual discharge from the service.

This is the story of a group of G.I.s who went through M.A.S.H. units and were evacuated to Japan for hospitalization and eventual return to their units.

The time was early March, nineteen hundred and fifty two and in Korea, the fighting was still going strong between the North Koreans and Chinese on one side and the United Nations forces on the other.

Charlie Fenner was a First Cavalry soldier and he was proud of that Combat Infantry Badge on his chest. He had mixed emotions about that Purple Heart in his duffle bag and the other ribbons.

He'd been wounded on an attack on a big hill they called Old Baldy and after a couple of months in the army hospitals, some surgery, and a lot of plasma, he'd made it through the rehabilitation process and now he had orders to report back to his old outfit.

1st Platoon, Able Company, 1st Batallion, 7th Regiment, 1st Cavalry Division, United States Army. The Division had practically been wiped out in the fighting earlier, and because of the high casualty rate, the entire division had been declared "combat inefficient," and evacuated to Sapporo, Japan, on the northern island of Hokkaido, for reorganization and training.

Private First Class Charlie Fenner had been riding on a train for 36 hours.

Charlie plunked his heavy barracks bag down near the doorway to Barracks 264. An Army jeep had brought him directly from the train station and now Charlie opened a duffle bag he had been carrying and removed from it a battered old bugle. He took the mouthpiece for the bugle from his pants pocket where he had put it earlier to warm it up. Now he put the mouthpiece in place in the bugle and brought the bugle to his lips as he threw open the barracks door. He blew hard and the bugle let out a loud ungodly sound.

Charlie walked inside the barracks a few steps and then he blew into the bugle once more. Again it let out a loud eerie sound.

"It's that son-of-a-bitch Charlie Fenner," one of the soldiers cried out.

"It's Fenner," another shouted and as the word passed, a dozen excited G.I.s ran forward and grabbed Charlie, hugging him and knocking his cap to the floor. Charlie simply could not keep up with all the hands that were offered for shaking.

One of the G.I.s took the bugle from Charlie's hand. "You got it, Charlie," he said. "You got that fuckin' Chinese bugle that drove us nuts every night in Korea. Great!"

"Yeah," Charlie laughed. "I got that bastard with the bugle just before I got hit."

Someone broke out a bottle of whiskey they had been saving for a special event. Having Charlie back in the bunch was that very special event. All of the men took a welcome drink as the bottle was passed from one glad hand to another.

P.F.C. Charlie Fenner had arrived from the hospital and rejoined his friends in Able Company. To be with your buddies again was something to celebrate. It was like being home again!

A buddy went out and picked up Charlie's barracks bag, came back and walked down the aisle with Charlie close by his side. The long room was lined on each side with Army cots and under each stood a pair of well-shined combat boots as straight and stiff as though someone had yelled, "tenshun!" The bare wooden floor was scrubbed to a near white color. Rifles adorned the center aisle and it was evident that every M-1 rifle there could have passed the toughest inspection. At the foot of each cot a foot locker stood in perfect alignment. The room looked sharp, really sharp, strictly infantry, with spit and polish from the floor to the ceiling.

They were a rough bunch of men, some were hairy, all were horny, most of them smelled badly at times, but Charlie was glad to be back among his friends.

God knows they'd earned a rest from that desperate fighting in Korea.

Charlie still had a bit of shrapnel in his thigh but the doctors at the M.A.S.H. Unit had removed all they could and subsequent inspection at the hospital determined that it would be best to leave it alone. When you considered what his body and mind had endured, Charlie was in pretty good shape as he cheerfully made his way to an empty upper bunk near the rear of the barracks. A tall, lanky private was lying on the lower bunk and he looked up as Charlie approached.

"Is this one taken?" Charlie asked.

"No, but it is now," the G.I. answered as he swung up out of his bunk and offered his hand to Charlie with the friendly greeting, "Hi, I'm Max."

"I'm brand new in this outfit," Max explained. "Still wet behind the ears, I guess. I just arrived overseas."

Max looked at the bugle on Charlie's cot. "What's with the bugle?" he asked. "I heard you blasting that thing when you came charging through the door. What's it all about?"

Charlie laughed as he leaned his shoulder against the bunk. "Psychological warfare! When we were in Korea and the Chinks used to blow those damned bugles all night long and they would drive us nuts. They had us expecting an attack every moment for awhile. We didn't dare go to sleep for fear they were on their way over."

"So how did you get the bugle?"

"Just lucky," Charlie grinned. "We were on Old Baldy and I just threw a grenade into the right bunker. Then I saw this guy with the bugle come running out of there and I nailed him with one shot."

Just then a line of G.I.s came back to watch as Charlie started unpacking his bag. One of them stuck out three dollars, "Here's the money I owe you, Charlie."

"And here's mine," another offered.

"Wait a minute, guys," Charlie said with a puzzled look on his face. "I sure need the money, I haven't been paid in a month, but what's if for?"

"Our beer ration," one of his buddies offered. "Did you forget?" The men laughed as one answered for the group, "First you took all of our money away from us in that last poker game and then you turned around and bought the beer ration for the whole company. Did you forget? We sure as hell haven't."

"Hey, that's right, I sure did," Charlie replied. "Thanks guys, I sure can use it. I'm really broke. I've been lining up every morning at the Red Cross office in the hospital just to get a pack of cigarettes. This money sure will come in handy."

At least a dozen G.I.s came forward and put money in Charlie's hand or threw it up on his bunk. With a sound of sadness in his voice a corporal commented, "You won't get all of your money back, Charlie, some of the guys didn't make it out of there. Those that aren't dead went to State-side hospitals."

"Yeah, tough, I know. But I really didn't expect to get any of my money back." Charlie broke into a smile. "The only reason I bought all you guys drinks is cause I didn't want to drink alone!"

Charlie was just getting his things settled when someone from the front of the barracks yelled, "Hey Fenner, Charlie Fenner, they just called over the 'Bitch Box.' As Charlie sorted the voice out of the babel it continued, "The old man wants you right away."

"The Captain?" Charlie asked. "What does he want?"

"I don't know, but you better get your butt over there pronto."

Still limping a little, Charlie went straight over to the Orderly Room and First Sergeant Fielding greeted him with a smile of recognition and motioned for him to go right on into the Captain's office. Captain Benson returned his salute and put him at ease, but went right to the point. "Charlie, you were a damned good rifleman, one of my best. I put you in for a Bronze Star for knocking out that machine gun position." As though searching for the right words he slowly lit a cigarette, then continued. "What I have to tell you now makes me very unhappy."

A frown passed quickly over Charlie's face. "What's that, sir?"

"I just got a call from Headquarters," the Captain replied as he stood and walked slowly around his desk and put his hand on Charlie's shoulder. "Your days as an Infantry Soldier are over. That wound you received has disqualified you from rifleman's duties. You've got to report to Headquarters right away for reassignment. You're a 'B' physical profile now unfit for a combat line outfit."

Charlie was stunned, he could feel a sense of frustration and anger starting to build up within. In fact, as the thought sunk in, he got mad, awfully mad and blurted out, "I'll be damned if they'll stick me with one of those lousy office jobs. They're not making a fag out of me!" To a combat soldier, anyone in an office job was a fag--a damn weak, pimply faced freak. It wasn't a job for him.

"I'm sorry about this Charlie," Captain Benson explained. "I really hate to lose you, but I can't change the whole army the way I'd like to. You'd better trot on over there and see what it's like. You might like it."

Half under his breath Charlie's lip formed one word, "Shit!" But the look on the Captain's face told him that the meeting was over. He snapped to attention, saluted and reluctantly returned to his barracks feeling as though he had been wounded by the enemy all over again.

Charlie and his buddies were infantry soldiers, every one of them, and each had tasted the experience of actual combat with the enemy. For this, they had all been awarded a C.I.B., a Combat Infantryman's badge. It was a blue medal about 3 inches long with a silver antique rifle embossed on it. The medal was surrounded by a silver wreath and it was to be worn above all the other medals on the uniform. That medal separated the men from the boys in the eyes of those who wore it.

The medal meant a lot to most of them, but there was something else, something deep inside, that every combat rifleman felt. It was hard to describe. A certain feeling of virility, as if each had entered the noble ranks of the gladiators. To each of them, from then on, every job in the army was secondary, somehow less than important. It was the feeling of specialness deep down inside each of these men that established an invisible bond not breakable even by death.

When he entered the long room his buddies could tell by the look on his face that they better not say too much. As he slowly repacked his meager belongings his feeling for his buddies was already creating an empty space in his chest and they all understood when he hoisted the bag to his shoulder and tried to act nonchalant with a brief "Sayanara." Reluctantly Charlie headed for the Headquarters office.

A P.F.C. directed him to the Personnel section where a First Lieutenant named Walters greeted him. Lieutenant Walters was already studying Charlie's 201 file and smiling with satisfaction.

"So you know how to type, do you, Private?"

Charlie was not impressed with Walters. He was just a little too effeminate. "A typical Personnel officer," Charlie thought.

"No, I don't know how to type," Charlie lied. "It's been years since I've even seen a typewriter."

"That's OK," the lieutenant replied as he gave Charlie some papers and a pretentious smile, neither of which Charlie liked. Then he continued, "There is a refresher course starting next week over on Eta Jima. We can get you there just in time."

"Eta Jima?" Charlie asked. "Where the hell is Eta Jima?"

"South, soldier, way south, far away from this cold, ice and snow. Way down south."

"Listen Lieutenant, if it's all the same to you, why don't we just forget this 'B' profile bullshit?" Charlie said. "I'll go back to my infantry outfit where I belong."

"I'm afraid that's out of the question, Private. You are physically unfit for infantry duty. You infantry riflemen are the glory boys, aren't you? You think the rest of us are second class, don't you?"

"I didn't say that," Charlie said.

"No, you doggies never say it. Well, Private, your days of glory are over. Your wounds make you unfit for glory. You get it?" The Lieutenant stared at Charlie and finally Charlie replied, "I don't see..."

"You don't have to see," the Lieutenant continued. "Now listen, you can take this thing either of two ways. You can go along with it and we'll send you to school if you cooperate, or, you can try to give me a hard time and you'll end up in the stockade. Do you understand, Private? Which will it be?"

Charlie didn't like the way the Lieutenant put it, but he figured the way the old Army routine works he might as well go along for the ride. He didn't like the deal at all, but what could he do? "I'll take the school," he said. "Since you put it that way."

The Lieutenant gave Charlie a sweet, smug smile. "Good. Take these papers right over to the supply shed and draw a full issue of kakis."

"Kakis!" Charlie exclaimed. The snow outside was six feet deep in places, the temperature was two degrees below zero and this nut was talking about getting a lightweight summer uniform. Charlie decided he didn't like the Lieutenant any more when he left than when he first came in.

The following morning Charlie delivered himself into the waiting hands of the U.S. Army Transportation Corps. Through some miracle and a little help from the Almighty he arrived at Kure, Japan about four days later. He wasn't sure how many days later it was but it couldn't possibly be as long as it seemed. The excitement of viewing Mt. Fuju and that lost wild weekend in Toyko had helped to break up the monotony. Somewhere on that endless train ride he struck up acquaintances with three other G.I.s caught in the same predicament that faced him. PERSONNEL MANAGEMENT SCHOOL their orders read.

"Sounds like training grounds for 'the girls,' isn't that what they call those pansies in personnel?" his friend Louis grumbled.

Louis Peltier was from the 24th Division and got his wounds on Pork Chop Hill and had a stiff shoulder to show for it. "Class 'B' Profile they call it," Louis kept on. "Not bad enough to get discharged they say, but too bad to go back as a dogface in my old combat outfit."

Ben Reardon nodded in agreement, "And it takes a 'B' Profile a hell of a long time to get stateside. You only get half as many rotation points as a dogface." Ben had a pretty little woman and a new son he hadn't even seen yet, back home. A few pieces of shrapnel here and there wasn't enough for a ticket home.

"I guess we're all class 'B's'," Frank Tucker agreed. "If we were back home we'd all pull 4-F, but not now. They've got us in their claws and are not about to let us go." Tucker explained how he got his ticket for the free train ride. "Got it in the knee. Same damned knee I broke playing football in high school. I think it's better now since I got hit than it was when they drafted me. Seems to bend a hell of a lot easier, at least. 'B' Profile, hell, I think them medics got Bees in their heads, a bunch of Sons of Bs, that's what."

When the train finally pulled into Kure, the four new friends managed to slip away from the inefficient U.S. Army Transportation Corps long enough to heist a few drinks of Asahi beer before reporting to the dock for the boat trip to the island of Eta Jima, where it was supposed to be so warm and beautiful.

Eta Jima was located on the Inland Sea just six kilometers south of Hiroshima and was established as a Japanese Naval Academy in 1888. Four years later a two-storied Red Brick Building was constructed for living quarters and study rooms for the midshipmen. The huge building accomodated up to 500 students. In 1917 the Massive Ceremonial Hall was built at a cost of over $500,000 and that at a time when you could stock an entire store with Japanese products for about $25.00. The DAI KODO section of the building accommodated 2,000 for special events and graduation ceremonies. The building was the first on the base made of fine granite, produced from Kurahashi Island located just south of Eta Jima.

In 1937 the three storied concrete building known as the E.M. Student quarters was completed. This was to be the temporary home of the students of the Personnel Management Class.

In 1945 the entire school had been turned into a hospital by the 308 General Hospital Unit of the United States Army soon after the surrender of Japan. In 1945 and 1946 the 41st and 24th United States Infantry Divisions had occupied the island and then from 1946 to 1949 the Australian Army occupied the site. It is rumored that it was through the constant pleas of the local Island girls that the Americans had returned and, when the Austrailians had departed, the Island was again turned into a training school. It was always a question as to whether the G.I.s learned more in school or in town after dark.

Before reporting to the boat Frank made his usual quick, totally impersonal survey and was assured that there were a lot of available girls on the island. "Toxan Musamae," (a lot of women) he gleefully reported, rubbing his hands together in earnest expectation. "Toxon moose, toxon beerhalls, toxon overnight passes, toxon everything. You know that 'R and R' the Army sends guys on for Rest and Recuperation, well men, we are in for some exciting 'I and I.' Those two big I's are for Intoxication and Intercourse."

"Is that all you can think about, drinking and whoring around?" Ben asked. "Haven't you got a girl back home?"

"I've got a whole passel of American women, but you could take the whole bunch of them and put them together and you still wouldn't have anything to compare with the way these Japanese broads know how to put it out." Frank laughed.

"I guess I'll have to take your word for that Frank, maybe I'm just chicken," Ben commented with a longing in his groin. "It might be OK for you single fellows but I've got too much to go home for to get burned out over here."

Frank led the way as they all walked down the dock and up the gangplank to the waiting P.T. boat that had been converted into a personnel carrier. It was fast and could carry 25 passengers without straining. Five other G.I.s, all wearing Combat Infantry Badges and Purple Hearts were already waiting patiently in their seats.

You guys 'B' Profiles, too?" Frank asked.

"Yeah, man, can you imagine us as pencil pushing clerks? A bunch of Dogface pencil pushers," replied Boots, also known as P.F.C. Henry Washington Smith. The name was a carryover from the days when his ancestors were slaves brought over from Africa.

Boots had wasted no time while waiting for the rest of the G.I.s to get their carcasses on board. He had made a quick tour of the high powered boat. That was one of the things that really turned Boots on--big powerful engines. He was good at fighting too. Two big scars on his upper arm proved that he'd been to Korea and back.

"What a horrible thing to do to a man. Trying to make a clerk out of him. It's downright demoralizing," Boots lamented.

"Don't try to cry on my shoulder, Fella," Frank barked. "I'm in the same boat."

"Yeah, I guess we sure are all in the same boat in more ways than one," Charlie chimed in, as he patted the side of the speedy P.T. boat. "We've all got 'B' Profiles, Combat Infantry Badges and Purple Hearts and the Army says we are not good enough for them anymore. Unfit. So do they discharge us? Hell no! That's too simple, they want to retrain us. Well, I'll tell you guys this, they're going to have a sweet time trying to make a fag out of me. If I'm unfit for combat they'll find out I'm unfit for everything."

"You know, it's pretty damn funny," Frank added. "When I was a civilian all them Army posters said 'Join the Army, be a man.' Well, I went along with it and joined up. Then this character comes along and tells us about Basic Training and says that it will separate the men from the boys. When I got basic I figured I had it made. I thought it proved I was a man. Then they tell you that you aren't a man 'til you go overseas. So over I come. When I get to Toyko some wise ass says you gotta go to Korea and earn a Combat Infantry Badge before you can be a real man. It's like there's no end to it. So I get the Combat Infantry Badge and next some yahoo tells me that just being there ain't enough, I got to get in a tough battle and get my ass half shot off before I can call myself a real man. Now I sure didn't intend to go that far, but I did. So I'm laying in the hospital and feeling pretty good that I'm still alive and this Colonel comes in and gives me my Purple Heart and all and I'm sort of figuring that I'm a real man and I get to discussing it with this fellow in the next cot. He says, 'Hell no, you aren't a real man until you get some of this fine Japanese tail.' "

"So what happened?" the troops asked in unison.

"So I slip out of the hospital one night and Whammo! I figured that I qualified three times that one night."

"And...?" the troops asked.

"And then," Frank continued. "And then I get to talkin' to this sergeant about being a man and he says that you aren't really a real man until you get the clap."

"So what do you plan on doing?" Boots asked.

"I'm quitting," Frank said firmly. "I figure that if I got the clap that somebody would come up with one more requirement and then one more and one more. I'm quitting while I'm ahead. But just because some asshole doctor says that I'm unfit for the infantry it doesn't mean a damn thing. They aren't going to make a damn woman out of me sitting behind a desk. Unfit, bullshit. I'll show them unfit. If I'm unfit for my riflemen's job then I'm unfit for the whole damn army."

"You got it," Boots agreed. "I'm not about to start in clerking. Unfit, hell. I'll give them unfit. I plan on being the unfittest motha they ever saw."

Charlie laughed. "We are the Unfit Outfit. A damn personnel lieutenant told me that I was unfit for glory. Well, whatta ya say we show them what unfit really means."

"Yeah," Frank agreed. "That's it. From here on out we are the Unfit Outfit. The biggest bunch of fuckoffs that the United States Army has ever had to deal with."

The pact was sealed. The United States Army, with all of its vaunted Counter Intelligence Agents, was sadly unaware of the chaos that was about to be created by the Unfit Outfit.

No, the United States Army would never ever again be quite the same.

2

The Tourist

Frenchie took the truck as far as the depot and then he began to wander through Nara, forgetting for a while that he as a G.I. and assuming the role of a tourist. He'd been in the Nara Army base less than a week and the single three hour pass he'd received didn't give him a chance to see any of the famous sites he'd read about. Before he boarded that train he was going to have a real good look around. He summoned a young rickshaw driver.

"Where you go, G.I.? You want nice girlsan?" The driver knew what the young men usually had in mind, obviously.

"I want to see Nara," Frenchie replied. "I want to see everything there is to see. I haven't got too much time but I want you to show me the whole city."

"You lucky G.I. You got number one sight-see boy in Nara. I show you everysing you want, just three thousand yen, OK, G.I.?"

Frenchie consulted his wallet and then remembered something he had heard about rickshaw drivers. "Twelve hundred yen and not a yen more."

"Jo To, OK, G.I., twelve hundred yen Di, jobu. (all right)."

"Where do we go first?" Frenchie asked.

"First, we go to park," the driver said as he kicked at his three-wheeled bicycle's motor to get it started.

"You mean where the deer and the shrines are?" Frenchie asked, holding tight to the side of the seat.

"You plenty smart G.I.," the driver said. They headed through the main section of town and out towards the park. In a few moments they arrived. The park was beautiful, the trees were budding and a number of small spotted deer were running free. Ojii, the driver, directed Frenchie to several colorful temples and shrines. Frenchie had seen them before in books but now it was all coming to life before his very eyes. He fed the deer and then they climbed back on the rickshaw and headed for the Todaaji Temple. Here a giant Budda that was cast in the year 749 was on display, a towering

53 feet 6 inches high weighing some 452 tons. The Temple itself was said to be the oldest wooden structure in the world, founded in 607 A.D.

Frenchie carefully viewed each site, wishing he had more time but he had to keep moving along. Next on the list was the Kasuga Shrine, which was painted fire engine red and decked out with a variety of metal lanterns. Taking Ojii's advice Frenchie removed his shoes and went into several of the relic temples. A huge gong hung outside the temple and Frenchie watched the elderly Japanese perform the gong ringing ritual. The huge gongs ('tsuri gane') were struck from the outside by means of a large block of wood suspended by ropes. The old man would draw the wood back and let it swing forward crashing solidly into the bell and producing a resounding crash. Bells like this are found throughout Japan at Buddhist temples.

Frenchie waited until no one was near and then, no longer able to resist the impulse, he pulled the hammer of wood back and gave the gong a resounding crash. Ojii spotted Frenchie in the act and covered his muted laughter with his hand.

It was growing late. Frenchie was satisfied, he'd seen the sights he'd read about and now he was willing to go back to the train station. As they headed back to the station Ojii stopped his rickshaw near a small teahouse on a side street.

"What are we stopping for?" Frenchie asked.

"I like to buy you hot sake G.I. Most G.I. just want Girlsan and get dingy dingy (drunk). You like Japan's nice things. Before I go I like to buy you sake."

"Thanks a lot," Frenchie said. "I'd like that very much."

The sake was very hot and sweet, it tasted good to Frenchie and he bought the second round. When they finally arrived at the train station, Frenchie discovered that he had just missed his train. There was a train due in 10 minutes for Nagoya however. True, it was in the wrong direction, but hell, he'd read about the wonderful shrines in Nagoya for years, and Gifu was just a few miles from there. He could go to both places and get back to catch a train the next day. Surely one day wouldn't make a lot of difference and he might not get another chance to see those sights. He went up to the ticket counter and bought a ticket to Nagoya. A few moments later the train came roaring into the depot and he was on his way. He found a seat in the coach and suddenly discovered that the whole train seemed to be built on a miniature scale. His long legs just didn't fit between the seats. He sat close to the aisle and let them hang out.

As the train began to move he suddenly realized how hungry he was. A few minutes later the train stopped and when he noticed other passengers buying food from the merchants on the platform. He opened his window and held out a couple of hundred yen. Quickly two small men came running to the window, bowed and spoke rapid Japanese that Frenchie didn't even attempt to decode. "Yea," he said and the men took his two hundred yen and handed him a small brown crock, a tiny vase, a bowl of white rice and wooden chopsticks. Frenchie carefully placed everything on the seat beside him as the train started on its way. For a full moment he casually watched those around him to see how they went about eating. He wasn't really sure what he had purchased. The brown crock was very hot and steaming. The vase was also hot and the rice was covered with small pieces of raw fish. The men all seemed to be starting out with their chopsticks and the brown crock. He took the lid off the crock and after a careful examination he decided it was bean soup with noodles. Frenchie studied the way the others held their chopsticks and, after several bad starts, finally cornered a noodle and started in. He noticed the man were all making loud slushing sounds and remembered the curious custom he had read about in Japan. The more noise you made while eating the better breeding you were supposed to have. Certainly he wasn't going to be outdone and so he started in with real gusto. The soup was hot and delicious. He'd drink a little soup and then casually snag a bit of rice from the bowl. The fish tasted great. Imagine eating raw fish. Well, he had eaten a lot of raw oysters back in the States so what was so different about raw fish? When he'd finished the soup, fish and rice, he felt much better. Now to investigate the vase. He took a sip and smiled. Sake. Hot sake. This was the way to travel. Just like riding in a club car in the States. He followed the actions of the other passengers and placed his crock and bowl on the floor and sat back and enjoyed the hot sake. A half hour later the train made another stop and Frenchie bought another vase of sake.

By the time the train reached Nagoya, Frenchie had achieved the true spirit of a tourist. He had it all figured out. He would go straight to Gifu, spend the night, and the following day he could return to Nagoya and see the sights, then boarding the west-bound express he could merely claim he took the wrong train the day before. He got off the train at Nagoya and boarded an electric train headed for Gifu. Thirty minutes later he arrived.

Gifu was not an extremely large town but to Frenchie it was really special. He rushed out of the depot and headed down the main street. He'd only gone a couple of hundred yards when a shapely young girl eyed him quite deliberately and then getting his attention she spoke quite softly, "Doko E Ki No G.I.?"

"Huh?" Frenchie asked.

"Where you go, G.I.?" she asked, smiling in a soft feminine way.

"I want to see the birds," Frenchie replied. "The river with the birds."

"You want to come to my house?" she asked.

"No sir, I mean no maam, I want to see the birds, that's what I came here for."

"I show you birds then you come to my house?" she asked.

Frenchie thought it over a minute, she sure was a beauty and he was going to spend the night there.

"What kind of deal can we make?" he asked.

"How long you mean?" she asked.

"Well, I want to stay all night and I have to eat yet and most of all I want to see the birds."

"Two thousand yen, all night, OK, G.I.?"

"Does that include dinner?"

"You come to my house and I fix you number one chop chop."

"When do we see the birds?" Frenchie asked.

She smiled. "Birds just out after nightfall. First you come to my house and we make chop chop."

It sounded like a really good package deal to Frenchie. The most important thing was the birds but after all, she was a beauty and he really wanted to try everything they had to offer in Japan. She led him down the street a couple of blocks and after a few turns they came to a small place with bamboo walls. "This my house," she said proudly. After proper direction Frenchie removed his boots and went inside and sat on the floor. Her name was Hatsuyo, Frenchie discovered. Gracefully, she moved about the room and she prepared a delicious sukiyaki meal on a Hibachi (a small coal stove). Carefully she blended the poy, water, sugar, vegetables, bean curd and then finally a macaroni-like substance called shirataki. Then slowly turning the small pieces of pork she had added, she allowed the mixture to simmer on the hot coal fire. About a half hour later the exact moment for serving had arrived and with great grace she served Frenchie a large portion. Frenchie ate his fill and then topped it all off with a cup of steaming green tea. He felt good now, really good. Several pillows made the Tatami (mat floor) seem quite comfortable. Hatsuyo removed the dishes and quietly took a seat beside Frenchie. She looked very sweet and young. She spoke softly, "Maybe one more hour before birds come out, you want somesing else maybe?"

Frenchie was suddenly aware that he was alone with a very desireable young girl. She was so sweet and cooperative and willing that he really didn't know how to act. He started to say something but stopped. He looked at her soft neck and smooth skin and felt his pulse quicken.

"You want to say somesing?" she asked.

"Ya," he said. "That sure was some meal you cooked."

"You like?" she asked, smiling happily.

"I sure do like, in fact I like you too."

"I happy you like."

He moved his pillow a little and sat across from her. He reached out and took her hand in his, then, on an impulse he kissed it. Quickly he slid closer to her and took her in his arms and kissed her, a long warm kiss. Her breath quickened and she whispered in his ear, "you want somesing?"

"Very much," he said.

"I want somesing too."

An hour later she had to remind him of the birds. "Oh ya, the birds, we've got to see the birds."

They quickly dressed and after a short walk they arrived at the bank of the river. "We get boat," Hatsuyo explained. "I know boat man and he no charge us."

"That's great," Frenchie said.

"Just charge if we want sake."

"Well I guess I can afford a little sake," Frenchie agreed.

The boat was big enough for a half a dozen passengers. One other couple was already aboard. In a few moments the small gasoline engine was started and they slowly drifted out into the river. Many other small boats were already out on the river and their colorful lanterns made a beautiful sight.

Soon the firecrackers began popping. Distant drums could be heard and soon the bright fires on the Cormorant boats came into view. Flotillas of small boats came closer and closer and now he could see them, a dozen on each boat. Just like those in the picture hanging above his bed when he was a boy. All his life he wanted to see the Cormonants. Now they were right there, large sea ravens on lines controlled by experts on the bow of each boat. The large birds had rings around their necks making it impossible for them to swallow the larger fish. The birds plunged in and gobbled ayu (smelt-like fish) until their bills couldn't contain any more fish and then the fishermen pulled them back on the boat and emptied their catch in waiting boxes. Thus relieved the birds plunged back into the water and quickly gobbled another load. Frenchie had seen a lot of different styles of fishing but this topped them all. Cormorant fishing had been going on for centuries. The birds were carefully trained and each keeper of the lines was a master, carefully controlling each bird and yet somehow, always avoiding a tangled line. Frenchie sat and gazed at the spectacle for more than an hour without saying a word. Hatsuyo bought them some sake and they drank it silently. He snuggled a little closer to her and squeezed her hand in his. The moon shined brightly on the river and Frenchie suddenly wished he could stay there forever. A little later the boat quietly floated ashore and the sightseer and his faithful guide returned to her house. Certainly Frenchie would never forget Gifu and Oh Yeah, they had birds there, too.

The following morning Frenchie awoke and remembered he was A.W.O.L. Hatsuyo prepared a fine breakfast of rice, bean curd soup, seaweed, smoked salmon and pickles. She topped it all off with a hot pot of tea. Frenchie was kind of mystified by the combination but was determined to try the Japanese customs. He was surprised at how good everything tasted. Hatsuyo certainly could cook, Frenchie decided, and that was one of her less notable talents. Frenchie knew he must get on the train to Nagoya early that morning if he hoped to see the sites. It took him more than an hour to say goodbye to Hatsuyo. He kissed her many times and finally left the house and ran all the way to the station. The train arrived in a few minutes and he was off to Nagoya. They had travelled only a few miles when suddenly Frenchie felt lonely. He hadn't had that feeling since his plane took off from New Orleans on the flight to Seattle. Now it was there again, eating away at him, making him feel so very much alone.

When he arrived in Nagoya he had a couple of vases of sake and then he started out to see the sights. He caught a train for the short ride to the Ise-Shima National Park. He saw the Grand Shrine of Ise near the seacoast town of Toba, the oldest and most important shrine in Japan. He saw the Sacred Bronze Mirror which is claimed to have been given to mankind by the Sun Goddess. It seemed quite unimportant. In fact nothing really interested him. He headed back to Nagoya and went into a small sake house and started drinking. He thought about Hatsuyo and for some reason he thought about his mother. He continued drinking.

Fortunately before he was too drunk to ambulate, he went to the station and checked the train schedule. There was a train going to Kure in just 30 minutes and Frenchie was on it. With a little luck he would arrive in plenty of time for the beginning of class.

3

Dippin' In

P.F.C. Thomas C. Gomez, United States Army. A decorated warrior. Citations--Combat Infantry Badge, Purple Heart, Korean Service Ribbon with one battle star. P.F.C. Thomas C. Gomez--drunkard. P.F.C. Thomas C. Gomez--coward.

Tom Gomez figured he was a pretty tough cookie when he was drafted into the United States Army, a fighter. Tom started fighting when he was just five years old growing up in a tough section of New York.

Then he was assigned to an infantry company with the 24th Division and after a month on the line, their outfit was sent up Heartbreak Hill.

The unit waited there a whole day and night before they were ordered up and, for a day and a night, a parade of dead and wounded were carried in a line that went directly past where his group was waiting for orders to attack.

The life expectancy of a machine gun crew, on an attack such as this, was about thirty seconds.

This was Tom's first real test in combat and certainly he was scared. Being pulled out of his regular rifle squad at the last moment didn't help his confidence either. And then, finally, when they were ordered into the attack, his original rifle squad was ordered in first and a Chinese mortar had come in right on target killing all of Tom's buddies, just as he was headed up the hill with the machine gun crew.

What happened after that P.F.C. Tom Gomez really didn't know for sure. He remembered running up the hill and feeling weak with fear. The heavy cans of ammo became heavier with every step. Still with a supreme effort, he managed to stay up with his machine gunner.

When they had reached the first crest of the hill he helped set up the gun and his gunner managed to fire nearly a whole belt of ammo when the mortar fire started coming in.

At that point, P.F.C. Tom Gomez went crazy with fear. All that he could remember is that he ran. He could not remember how or why but finally, moments later a medic had actually tackled him and shouted "Hold it, man, you are wounded and bleeding badly."

As it turned out, Tom Gomez had a shrapnel wound in his left shoulder but the wound was not serious, at least not as serious as what was going on inside P.F.C. Tom Gomez. Tom was ashamed.

Later, at the M.A.S.H. unit, he learned that, except for him, the entire machine gun crew had been killed by mortar fire. Because he had run like that, Tom felt that he was a coward.

God, how he wanted to try again, just to prove to himself that he could stand up to the enemy.

At the hospital--in Kobe General Hospital in Japan, he'd talked to the doctors about his feelings and a psychiatrist explained to Tom that what he'd done was not at all unusual, but that wasn't good enough for Tom. Deep down inside he felt rotten about himself and perhaps that was one of the reasons that he drank so much. When he drank enough, he forgot about Korea and about his being a coward.

And now the army was shipping him to clerk's school and robbing him of the chance to redeem himself in combat.

Tom Gomez was sitting in the train station in Kobe, Japan, feeling rotten about being in the army and about life in general, waiting for his train. It was scheduled for 1500 and Nara was about 130 miles west of Kure where he would board a U.S. Navy boat for a short ride to Eta Jima.

It was still thirty minutes until train time and so Tom walked out of the train station and looked up and down the street for a bar.

A drink, he thought, might put him in a better mood for that long train ride. The way trains moved in Japan, Tom knew it would take many hours for them to reach Kure.

Besides, he wanted to pick up a fifth of whiskey or two for the journey.

He didn't have to look long. Just two blocks from the train station he found a small sake house and he sat down and ordered a double shot of Japanese whiskey and a hot vase of sake for a chaser.

That was exactly what it took to get him started and the young girl who waited on him kept the drinks flowing throughout the afternoon and far into the night.

Just before midnight, P.F.C. Tom Gomez decided that he'd better get back to the train station. He was so drunk by then that he was staggering badly.

The area near the train station was an old run-down area of the city and they had no plumbing facilities whatsoever.

Farmers in that area had a working agreement with the local shops where by much needed organic fertilizer was collected in a barrel and early this morning the barrels were emptied by an ox-driven cart known as the Honey Bucket Wagon. The barrels themselves were stored in pits in the street and the pits were covered with boards. That evening, however, a board had been moved and P.F.C. Tom Gomez in his staggering way, as if directed by radar, fell right into the barrel. The terrible stench partially sobered him up and he struggled a moment before pulling himself from the barrel. He was covered from head to toe. He heard a train whistle and made a dash for the station. Running quickly through the station he spotted the train about to leave and with a wild leap he went sailing through the open vestibule door. This train, loaded with American soldiers who had just arrived from the States, was a special troop train and it had stopped for coal and water for its locomotive. It was not scheduled to take on new passengers and the G.I.s were quietly sleeping in the upper and lower berths and Tom crept silently down the aisle. He noticed the G.I.s clothing hanging by each berth. First he spotted a cap and taking his own off he quietly traded. He walked a little further down the aisle and removed his filthy tie and shirt. He traded those items with another sleeping G.I. On further he traded trousers and as he reached the last cot, he traded shoes. Now completely redressed, he walked through the next car and in the third sleeping car he found an empty upper berth and proceeded to make himself at home.

P.F.C. Tom Gomez laid there in the darkness and suddenly he started laughing. It was a quiet laugh to begin with, but it built in intensity until it was a loud roaring laughter.

"Dipped in shit," he cried out and he laughed even louder. "I've been dipped in shit." He cried out to the darkness. The darkness did not answer and so, eventually, he went to sleep.

The following morning he arrived at Eta Jima. After a couple of hours in the shower he felt like a new man. He was right on time, classes started the next day.

4

Leisure

Melvin Tuttle had always been, 'the little guy,' everyone pushed him around and there wasn't a thing he could do about it, he no longer cared. That was all behind him now. The Army had changed all of that. Now he was a new man, hereafter, he could give the orders and these lowly privates would have to obey them. He was a Corporal and he had a couple of stripes to prove it. He had sewn them on in his spare moments aboard ship, coming overseas.

Fresh out of Leadership School, the Army's School that was supposed to make real leaders out of whatever came in the front door. He'd practiced hard on giving orders in front of the mirror. He had barked, growled and yelled out the orders. "Hup, hope, three, four! Dress it up! Eyes forward!" He knew it all down to the last detail and now the Army was sending him to another school, "Personnel Management School," the orders read, and now here he was on the Island of Eta Jima.

He walked down the long hallway until he found the Orderly Room, stopped, straightened his tie, pulled his shoulders back and strutted in.

"Priv, er, I mean Corporal Melvin A. Tuttle reporting for training, Sir!" he stammered as he snapped to attention.

"Corporal, do you see these stripes?" Sergeant Bill Riley drawled as a bored expression filled his face.

"Yes Sir, Sergeant," Tuttle replied in his most military manner.

"Then quit calling me Sir!" Riley fumed. "I'm an enlisted man and you don't call enlisted men, Sir."

"Yes Sir, Uh, I mean yes, Sergeant," the Corporal mumbled.

"Well take those shiny new clothes of yours in that shiny new duffle bag and find a sack in room 214. You're the only non-com in that Personnel Management Class, so I guess that means you will be in charge of them. They're a fine bunch of guys. Too bad they got the same raw deal I did by getting classified 'B' profile. Shit, I'll bet a little pip-squeak like you has an 'A' profile, haven't you, Corporal?"

"Yes Sir, I mean, yes indeed Sergeant," the meek little Corporal answered.

"Damn it, Corporal, don't call me Sir."

"OK Sergeant, I'm sorry, it's just that we called all non-coms, Sir, at Leadership Training School."

"Leadership School! So that's where you got those stripes, is it? Well I'll bet you have one sweet time with those 10 displaced doggies, corporal. They don't cotton up to the Leadership School way of soldiering, understand?"

"No Sir, I mean, Yes Sir!"

Now even slow speaking Riley was getting fed up and his face began to show his anger. "Corporal, don't you ever call me Sir again. Now get your ass out of here and let me clue you in for your own sake, try to forget all those half-assed things they tried to teach you at Leadership School."

Tuttle turned and slowly walked out of the office with dejection written all over his face. He supposed that since the Sergeant was so cold on the word Sir, he couldn't expect the fellows in the classes to call him Sir. Oh, well, he was still the non-com and this was his first real opportunity to command. He walked quickly down the hall and after two turns around the corridor, he found room 214.

It was a big room with windows all along the back wall. There were 40 cots in all, four rows of 10 cots each and the mattresses on the first three rows were turned up indicating that they were unoccupied. The 10 cots along the back wall were unrolled and on each was a fully clothed G.I.

Corporal Tuttle sucked a big gust of air into his little five foot two frame in a vain effort to look five foot three, then walked stiffly back to the last aisle of cots.

"Men," he announced. "I'm Corporal Tuttle, your new non-commisioned officer. We're going to be attending classes together and I understand that I am to be in charge. First of all let's hop to it and get these beds made. No more smoking in bed. Let's look sharp men, we have lots of work to do."

Not one man stirred. The smoking continued until Frank broke the stillness to drop his butt on the floor and stomp it out. He only responded then because the cigarette was so short that it was about to burn his fingers.

Corporal Tuttle's face froze in utter confusion. This was not the way it was supposed to be at all. After staring at each man in shocked surprise, he turned on his heel and practically ran to Sergeant Riley's office.

"Sergeant," he blurted. "Those men are all guilty of insubordination."

"Corporal," Riley sighed with a look of disgust on his face. "Why don't you let me have a little peace and quiet? Now, you don't have to tell those fellows anything, they know the ropes. They can make that room perfect with their eyes closed. Just keep quiet and leave them alone. They won't bother you if you don't try to bother them. Come on, Corporal, forget that crap they taught you at Leadership School. Just go in there and take a cot and keep your damn mouth shut. They are big boys, they'll take care of themselves if you keep out of the way and leave them alone."

"Yes, Sir," Tuttle turned and started to march briskly back to room 214 but his pace slacked off as he approached the door. Tuttle thought, "That Sergeant doesn't know anything about leading men. He probably got his rank through some pull. I'll show him. I'll show them all. I'll do it the right way, the leadership way and these men will come through with flying colors." But when he finally got back to the room it was empty. The beds were made and everything was in order, ready for inspection.

After prolonged searching he finally found the men in the big elaborate marble lined latrine, squatted on the floor busily shooting craps. Some of them seemed to be taking turns and then getting up and walking into the back stall only to come back a few seconds later wiping their sleeve across their mouth. The group seemed to totally ignore Tuttle so he finally worked his way over to the back stall and peeked in only to spot a couple of empty whiskey bottles on the floor and a half full one on the top of the tank. He turned and looked at the laughing bunch of men moving about on the floor, his mouth hanging part way open, unable to speak.

"Well, man you gonna take a drink or not," Tom Gomez asked as he waited to see which way Tuttle was going to go. "If not, step out of the way and let a man in there."

Tuttle started stepping hesitatingly away from the stall as though the Devil himself was in the way no matter which way he went, "You can't drink here. It's against regulations."

"You mean it's against regulations if you get caught," Frank commented as he waited for Tom to finish, then he practically reached right over Tuttle's head to take the bottle from Tom's hand. "We don't get caught because we know what we are doing, Corporal. This is one of those days when anything goes. We get these days in the army when the only thing we have to do is arrive, get our bedding, make our beds and be available for duty the next day. Anyone dumb enough to stick around the barracks will be told to do some little house cleaning chores. But if we stay out of sight, anything goes. If you're going to be part of our outfit you can join in the game, if not you better get your butt out of here and forget that you ever saw us."

"But what if the Sergeant finds out?" Tuttle wasn't about to give up his rightful position of dominance that easy.

"The Sergeant was the guy who tipped us off that no one would be coming near this latrine. He's a pretty good Joe. Used to be a combat medic in the First Division, got it in the gut and they made him a 'B' profile like the rest of us. He's going nuts on that job."

Charlie looked up from the floor. "This is our own private get acquainted party ballroom, now you gonna join in the fun or not?"

Tuttle looked defeated. "I think I'd better get back to the barracks. I've got to get my footlocker in shape and besides, it's still against Army regulations."

Several men on the floor chorused, "Get lost Corporal, or you'll be sorry you ever found us. We'll see you in the morning."

5

Their Leader

Captain Wesly Thompson was a veteran of World War Two. He made sure everyone he met knew it. Actually he had used every angle possible to avoid miltary service, during the Second World War. He was fairly successful at it too for a while. He should have been, he tried everything. It was not until early in 1945 that the Draft Board finally grew tired of his many excuses for remaining a civilian and drafted him into the U.S. Army. You have to give him credit for his efforts though, he contacted a close relative who had a lot of influence on Officer's Candidate School assignments, and he got in there.

Whether through a little conniving, some dumb luck, or a quirk of fate, he graduated as a full-fledged 90 day wonder, a second Lieutenant, the day before Japan surrendered.

Through another series of maneuvers, he managed to transfer to the National Guard and after attending only two weeks of training on an off year, when he somehow ran out of excuses, had raised himself to the rank of Captain. Korean Peace Action caught him totally unprepared and he was quickly activated into military duty and shipped overseas without further training. Through a series of mysterious miracles that seemed to follow him everywhere, he was not shipped to Korea like most of the others, but to Eta Jima. To the surprise of everyone but Captain Thompson and his favorite gods, he became the School Administration Officer, in charge of all enlisted men attending the school.

His only previous experience in leadership was in Women's Wear at a Franklins' Department Store where he had three salesladies under him. He may have had more women than that under him but that was all that he got paid for.

His friends used to tease him about being in Women's Wear, frequently implying that they suspected he was a fag.

"What would they say if they could see me now?" he often asked himself as he admired the view in the full-length mirror he had had installed in his office. "Captain in the United States Army."

He had just removed his folded handkerchief from his pocket and started to proudly polish his already glittering silver shoulder bars when the door abrubtly swung open. He quickly turned away from the mirror and tried to act as though he were doing something worthwhile for a change. But his voice was almost pleading like a little kid with his hand caught in the cookie jar, "Sergeant Riley, how many times have I told you to knock, before entering?"

Riley acted like he hadn't seen the Captain preening himself in front of the mirror. "I've got some more of those damn papers for you to sign Captain. Papers, papers and more papers. Six copies of everything, I just wish I could get back in the First Division and do something useful."

The Captain, who was delighted that he was not in the First Division, replied, "You've said that before Sergeant and I've told you before that my school, er, our school is serving a very useful function. We are training men for very important work. We can't all be on the front lines. As you may have forgotten, I was in World War Two, I feel I've earned my right to this non-combat position."

"You don't have to tell me about it Captain, I was in it too." Riley remarked dryly as he disgustedly threw the papers on the Captain's well-polished desk. He turned to leave when the Captain's voice caught up with him. "I want you to remember that I am a Commissioned Officer, Sergeant, from now on I want to see you show more respect for my rank."

Riley's reply fortunately was not heard as he was talking more to himself, "I want you to remember that I am a Commissioned Officer. Shit! He wouldn't make a scab on a real officer's fanny. He's a misplaced civilian, he wouldn't last one minute in the line outfits. If the Chinks didn't get him one of his own men would. Respect, Hell! I'll give him all the respect he deserves. Absolutely none."

A few minutes later the Captain marched through the outer office and down the hall of Quarters Building holding his head high. He liked the recognition that this trip gleaned from his subordinates. He let as many as he could know that he was about to perform the necessary function of holding reveille formation. He was awed by his own importance when the words, "Ten'shun" caused everyone to snap into a state of rigidity because of his very presence.

"Assembly report!" he roared the best he could, as he thought to himself, "Man, if those jerks back at Franklins' Department Store could only see me now."

"First class all present and accounted for," a voice reported.

"Second class all here and accounted for," another called out.
"Third class all here and accounted for."
"Fourth class all here and accounted for."
"Fifth class, one man AWOL," Little Corporal Tuttle reported importantly.
"Assembly dismissed," Captain Thompson yelled.
Frank turned to Tuttle and said, "Whadda you mean, one man is AWOL?"
"Peltier's not here," Tuttle replied.
"You know damn well, he's upstairs shaving. That makes him present and I just accounted for him."
"But he's not at formation," Tuttle argued.
"Formation hell," Frank countered. "If a fellow is around and you know he's around and then he's not AWOL. Everyone has a bad morning once in a while. We'll get enough fellows out here so that it looks like a formation. If a fellow is in town or something then OK, he might be AWOL, but if he's a little slow some morning and you know he is around, then he is present and accounted for."
Sergeant Riley walked rapidly over to where the two men stood arguing, and asked, "Who is AWOL?"
"No one is AWOL," Frank answered. "He's right there in the barracks shaving and Tuttle knew it. You wouldn't want him to show up the first day of class looking like a bum. He had a little upset stomach and headache so he slept in a few minutes. Must have been the excitement of his first day at school."
"That's right Corporal, if a fellow does not feel good and you or someone else can account for him, then don't report him AWOL," Riley turned to Frank and winked in agreement.
As Tuttle walked away Riley said, "Guess us old Class 'B' Profiles will have to stick together, huh, Frank?"
"Guess so Sarg, at least until we get these new fellows broken in right."
Breakfast was a real production as the largest class at Eta Jima was the Cook's School. They had an endless supply of food to experiment with and the students were the guinea-pigs. Breakfast was the best meal, after all how many ways can you mess up Corn Flakes? Eggs were cooked to order to an uncertain degree. The only sure thing about the arrangement was that you would invariably get someone else's order.
Later, well fed, the men assembled outside the Quarters Building for their first trip to class. Corporal Tuttle could hardly control his excitement as his imagination raced ahead. At last, he had his

very own squad to drill and he was going to drill them until he had the sharpest group on the whole base. Precision marching! At last his moment of glory was here. He sucked his lungs full of air and shouted, "Fall in!" The men did a reasonable imitation of coming to attention.

"About Face," the men turned around at their own individual speed, but at least they all turned to face the same direction.

"Fooor-warrrd, March!" They did not march. The men started walking like a bunch of college freshmen stolling across campus.

"Hup, hope, hip, four. Hup, hope, hip, four," Tuttle barked.

"What are you majoring in, Frank?" Ben inquired.

"You are not supposed to be at ease," a very frustrated Tuttle snapped, "You men are supposed to be marching at attention. Hup, hope, hip, four. Dress it up. Eyes forward, stand tall. Come on you guys, dress it up. Hup, Hope, Hip, four."

The men acted in perfect unison all right, but it was to tune Tuttle out. They kept on ambling.

Tuttle's frantic efforts continued. "Hup, Hip, Hope, Four. Hup, Hip, Hope, Four. Count cadence, Count."

"Is he really serious?" Ben asked. "He couldn't be." Frank laughed. As the men continued their leisurely stroll to the classroom, Corporal Tuttle continued barking orders at the group with as much effect as a little puppy barking at an elephant. After about 10 minutes walking and talking the men arrived at the Instruction Hall and fell out just before Tuttle commanded, "Fall out!"

He thought "That's better, they did that without arguing, they finally obeyed an order."

The Corporal decided the men needed a couple of days on the drill field and he would have them right in line.

After a smoke break the bell rang and the men reported to their classroom. The first hour was spent learning the curriculum: Army forms, Typing, Regulations, Military Justice, Insurance and a special class on Making Morning Reports. There were Army forms to fill out. "Press down hard men, to make sure the sixth copy will be legible!" The instructing Sergeant suggested, "Not that anyone is ever going to read them except some Corporal with nothing better to do." The Sergeant seemed nice enough but the subjects did not make much of a hit on anyone except Corporal Tuttle.

After an hour of lecturing they were given a smoke break. "Let's all go AWOL," Frenchie suggested.

"Yeh, then maybe we could all get kicked out of this mess the first day," Frank agreed.

"You fellows missed the boat," Louis confided, looking as if his sweepstakes ticket had just been picked. "We're gonna have a ball. We can spend all day studying those Army regulations and all night breaking them. All the time you're studying keep thinking of the ways we can bend the regulations for our own protection. When I was in Basic Training we had a fellow who made a career out of studying them regulations and how to get around them. He did just about anything he wanted and got away with it. If you learn what those regulations say and more important what they don't say, you can get away with murder. The minute anyone doesn't go by the book you can go to the Inspector General, the I.G., and he has to see that things go by the book. Nobody knows what the book says and so they break the rules. You can catch some of those big shots with an infraction and hold that over them, too. Once we learn the regulations we can use them to our own advantage."

"Hey, that sounds like the very idea we talked about when we talked about calling ourselves the Unfit Outfit," Ben remembered. Frank joined in by saying, "Then the Unfit Outfit is about to go into action, let's all major in regulations!"

Nine young eager voices bellowed in agreement then burst into laughter.

Tuttle practically ran up to the group, demanding, "What are you fellows up to now?"

Frank replied with a deadpan serious look on his face, "We've just agreed that it is to our advantage to study really hard so we can make the most of our visit here."

Tuttle relaxed, a look of satisfaction filled his face and the thought went through his mind, "Well, it's about time they began to get the spirit that I want them to have. Getting them to drill will be easy now."

The morning's classes went quicker after that, as the men took an unusual interest in the session on Army Regulations. At noon they fell out in front of the Instruction Hall, as they talked among themselves they decided that the Unfit Outfit would soon make the Hall of Instruction become known as the Hall of Destruction.

Tuttle assumed his most military posture and snapped, "Fall in" and was taken by surprise when the men came to attention in perfect ranks, chin in, chest out, eyes forward, gut in, looking like a crack drill team. Tuttle stood there in silent disbelief for a moment then with a l ook of immense satisfaction on his face, barked, "Right face." The troops carried his order out with precision.

Forward march, Hup, Hope, Hip, Four." It was like a dream for

Tuttle, his own private drill team. "Count cadence, Count."

"One two three four, one two three four," the men responded with an unusual snap to their voices. "To the rear march." The men executed the move brilliantly. "Double to the Rear. To the right Flank, March," followed by "Double to the Rear, to the left Flank, March, Squad Column Right, Right March."

It was too good to be true, like having the American Legion Drill Team performing at a Fourth of July Celebration. They were perfect.

Tuttle beamed. "I knew I could do it," his little chest puffing out proudly as he directed them towards the Power Building. The little Corporal was so proud and so overcome with joy that he could hardly contain himself. He gave another order to reassure himself that the men really were cooperating at last. "To the rear, march!" The men responded in perfect unison.

He checked again, just to be sure, "Count Cadence, Count."

"One two three four. One, two, three, four," they responded in a voice that left Tuttle just a little puzzled, so he tried again, "To the rear, march."

He was so delighted with his new found power that he decided to take the long route back to the barracks. He marched them around the Power Building hoping some of the officers would see how well he could command his group of men.

The grassy strip narrowed to a dirt path with the building on one side and a deep stream on the other. Tuttle had moved up to march proudly at the side of his men. As they reached the point where the road was the narrowest someone in the rear ranks ordered. "Column half left, do it!" The men pivoted smartly. All except Tuttle. There was no room for him to pivot or do anything else. Without laying a hand on him, he was pushed into the stream. The men pivoted again on an unspoken order and marched on. Eyes forward.

Tuttle's head bobbed up above the water and he screamed, "I didn't give that command, damn it." As he waded to shore he screamed, "Wait for me you guys. I'm your leader."

When he finally got back on the path, he started running after the squad, his wet clothes slopping water as he kept repeating, "Halt, damn it!" Apparently they did not hear him until nearly reaching the E.M. Quarters.

"Halt!" he screamed, the men came to perfect military halt in front of the doorway.

"Freeze!" he sneared, as he rushed around to stand in front of the group, expecting the men to stand at stiff attention.

"Fall out, men," someone in the rear of the ranks yelled and the men nearly trampled poor little Tuttle as they ran through the door, into the building.

"Just a minute, Fenner," Tuttle said, pointing to Charlie, as he walked briskly towards the door. "You're going to the captain's office with me. I saw you yell that order that pushed me in the ditch."

"Who, me?" Charlie responded, looking as innocent as he could under the circumstances.

"Yes, you," Tuttle growled.

"Whatever you say Corporal, but I'm not sure what you're talking about."

Tuttle marched just behind Charlie as they went up the stairs and into the Orderly Room where Sergeant Riley sat wishing he were somewhere else.

"What's wrong now, Tuttle?" He smiled as he noted Tuttle's soaked uniform and the look of dismay on the little man's face.

"I want to put this man on report, Sir," Tuttle demanded, his face white in contrast to his wet clothing.

"What for?" Riley queried.

"Insubordination."

"Insubordination?"

"Yes, Sir. He's shouting orders in the ranks and everything."

"He is?" Riley replied, a kind, rather motherly look spreading across his face and though his eyes belied his words, continued, "Well Corporal, there is only one thing that I suggest you do to show this man that you mean business. Take him out in back of the building and just beat the livin' shit out of him. Show him no mercy. Then he'll know that you are boss and won't stand for any of that monkey business."

Even more blood drained from Tuttle's little face as he looked up at Charlie's face and surveyed his huge football player's frame. "Thank you, Sir," he said weakly, his eyes now focused on the floor.

Charlie turned and looked down at Tuttle as he spoke with quiet authority. "Well Corporal, I suppose I'll just have to take my medicine."

Tuttle looked up out of the corner of his eyes for a long moment with the same feeling Custer's men must have had when they saw all of those Indians. Finally his voice faint with fear, "Well Private, I am going to be lenient on you this time. I've decided to let you off, but let this be a lesson to you." He turned and practically ran out into the hall.

Charlie looked back into the understanding eyes of the Sergeant, who said, "I'm sure this will be a lesson to somebody."

Charlie laughingly agreed. "That's what we are here for--to learn."

6

Persento

Frank Tucker knew all about Oriental women and he loved 'em. It had been five days since he arrived on the Island of Eta Jima and he was itching all over to get into town. The first opportunity that passes were available he skipped supper, shaved, took a shower, carefully pinned his combat ribbons on a clean, well-starched shirt, cocked his hat so that it reached down to his left eyebrow, signed the pass book and headed for town. It was 1830 when he went through the gate. 2400 was curfew. Lots of time to have a ball. He'd no sooner passed through the gate when he heard an old familiar chant. It was a girl. A pretty Japanese girl. Short, carefully dressed, an ample figure and a prettier smile.

"Where you go, G.I.?" she asked softly. "You come on my house, OK G.I.?"

"Me cherry boy," Frank lied.

"Me Cherry Girl too G.I. You come to my house and we have a good time, OK G.I.?"

"Not right now, Honey. You show me a good beer hall first, OK?"

"I get you beer in my house, you come-on OK?"

"Maybe I'll see you later, Honey; first I want to look the town over, and the talent too."

The girl turned and went back to her post outside the gate. Frank headed toward the sound of a noisy phonograph record. A big sign said "Tiger Bar" and Frank walked in and took a seat in a booth. A pretty girl came over and sat down with him.

"You want Biiru G.I.?"

"Ya, a beer."

"Kirin or Asahi?" she asked.

Frank shrugged and said, "You name it."

The girl returned in a minute with a quart bottle of Asahi Beer and a glass. She also sat a small flat paper cup full of light unsalted peanuts on the table. Frank gave her a nice new crisp 1000 yen note and she soon returned with 750 yen change. She sat down beside him as she put the money on the table. Frank put a cigarette in his mouth and before he could find his lighter the girl lit the cigarette for him and then carefully let the match burn. When it had burned near to her fingers she wet her fingers carefully, took the burned end into her wet fingers and then let the match burn entirely out. Having accomplished this without breaking the charcoal remains, the girl smiled happily and snuggled a little closer to Frank.

Frank took a sip of beer and the girl quickly filled his glass. The record player started up again, this time blasting out with a popular Japanese number, China Night. The girl took Frank's hand and held it while she gazed adoringly into his big blue eyes.

"You dance G.I.?"

"Sure doll, we dance," Frank got up and stumbled around the tiny dance floor, then he sat down, finished his beer, cocked his hat at the proper angle and headed for the door.

"Sayanara G.I," the girl called softly. "You come back again."

"Ya, sayanara," Frank said.

He walked along the narrow dirt road, passed a souvenir shop and then turned and walked into a second shop he came to. The shop keeper was an old man with a white goatee. He shuffled slowly from the rear of the shop when Frank entered.

"You want buy French Tickler, G.I.?"

"No, just looking," Frank replied, wondering if maybe they sold Japanese Ticklers in France.

"Nice present for your sweetheart back home, eh G.I.?" The old man held a silk scarf which was decorated with pictures showing 57 various ways to make love.

"That would go over like a lead balloon."

"How 'bout Ronson cigarette lighter made out of old beer can?"

"I've got nine of those already."

"Chopsticks? Sake glass? Pearls? Maybe you like real Japanese French postcards, very, very nice G.I., OK?"

"No," Frank said as he headed for the door. "I just wanted to look around. Allegato anyway."

Frank continued down the street, passing a tea house, a tiny liquor store, a cabaret, five more pretty girls, complete with invitations, another cabaret, two more souvenir stores and finally he came to another cabaret. He went in, drank two more quarts of beer, danced, ate peanuts, had his cigarette lit for him and then decided it was time to take the girls on the street a little more seriously. It sure wasn't like back home, where you took a girl to a movie, brought her a hamburg and then fought for what little you could get before you took her home. No fighting in this town. Just pay a few hundred yen and you were in business. It wasn't like paying for it in the States either. The gals in the States that did it for money were no fun. Strictly a business. On and off, pay your money, hit the road. These Oriental women were different. They made it seem like you were their lifetime lover. They really had fun and there was nothing dirty or illegal or wrong about it. It was legitimate and their only purpose in life was to make you happy. And they sure could make Frank happy. He cocked his hat and headed for the next block which appeared to be the busier end of town.

"Where you go, G.I.?" she asked.

Frank turned, took one look and decided, this was it.

"Just walkin'," Frank said, starting to turn away.

"OK, we walk, G.I. What's your name?"

"Frank."

"I'm Teriko. You call me Terry, OK Frank?"

"OK, Terry."

"You want to buy me cider, Frank?"

"Sure Terry, let's go into this place." Frank took Terry by the hand and they went into a small cabaret. He ordered one cider and one beer. They held hands and both of them seemed to feel good all over looking at one another. Frank finished his beer and his heart was pounding.

"We go to your house now, OK Terry?"

"OK Frank. You got 400 yen. No 400 yen and papasan get pisto."

"I got 400 yen."

They walked to the end of the street and turned down a narrow dirt road. Weaving in and out between a mass of tiny shacks they finally arrived at Teriko's place. Frank sat down and took his heavy boots off and laid them on a narrow ledge near the door. It was a busy house, several girls moved in and out and G.I.s were constantly coming and going. Terry took Frank into a small room and as he entered gave her four one hundred yen notes.

"Now Papasan no pisto," she laughed half seriously.

Frank put his arms around Teriko and held her close to him. She was soft and warm and wonderful. They sat down on the mat on the floor that was the Japanese style bed and soon they were locked in love. It was like a dream, fantastic, thrilling and it all seemed so right. The dream was ended much later by a loud knock on the door.

"That's papasan," Teriko whispered. "No more time, you go

back to camp now, almost curfew."

Frank looked at his watch. 2350. Ten minutes to get through the gate. He put his arms around Teriko and kissed her again. She held him close and kissed him on the face and neck and whispered softly to him, "Puresento." She took his hand and kissing him gave him something. He looked and stared in disbelief. It was his 400 yen.

Frank ran down the hall toward the door and heard Teriko as she softly called, "Sayanara."

He leaped through the door and reached for his boots. They were gone. He looked on the ground. He looked on the stoop. He called Teriko and they both looked. Papasan soon came out and joined in the search but the boots were nowhere in sight. Four minutes until curfew. He had to get back to camp or he would be AWOL. He started running down the street in his stocking feet.

"If I can just get through the gate, I'll have it made," he thought. "I'll just try to walk like I've got shoes on, that's all there is to it." He started practicing as he neared the gate, 100 feet to go. He was doing fine. Just march, that's it. Hup, hope, hip, four. That's it, swell. Ten feet from the gate. Quite a bunch of G.I.s, going through the gate, these MPs won't notice. Five feet. Two feet. Now he was walking right past the MPs. Suddenly he stepped on a sharp stone.

"OOOOOW!" he yelled, grabbing his foot and jumping around on the other.

"Hey Charlie, look at this guy. No shoes." The MP held his stick against Frank's chest.

"Out of uniform. Give him a D.R.," the other MP replied, bored with the whole procedure.

"What's a D.R.?" Frank asked.

"A Disorderly Report," the MP replied. "We've got to give you one."

The MP quickly filled out the report and gave Frank a copy.

"Your Commanding Officer will see you about this in the morning."

Frank limped to his quarters, found his cot in the dark, thought pleasant thoughts about Teriko, and went to sleep.

Captain Thompson sat behind his well polished desk shining the silver bars on his padded shoulder. He felt good this morning. Three D.R.s had been turned in and now he could exert a little authority. Frank knocked at the door and then marched into the office, reported and stood at attention.

"Oh yes," Captain Thompson said slowly, "You've got a D.R. for being out of uniform. Disgraceful, Private. Men have fought and died for that uniform and you don't even gave the decency to wear it properly."

"Well you see sir--"

"At ease Private. I don't want to hear any of your lame excuses. You understand, Private, if I choose I can have you court martialed for this offense, or, on the other hand, I can also allow you to take the provisions of Article 15."

"What are they, Sir?" Frank asked.

"Well Private, if you want to sign this paper stating that you choose Article 15, then I can do one of several things. I can put you on extra duty for one week. I can pull your pass or I can reduce you in rank one grade."

"I'll take Article 15," Frank replied.

"Then sign here," the Captain said, handing a paper across the desk.

Frank signed it.

Captain Thompson smiled. "I'm reducing you from Private First Class to Private, soldier."

"Listen Captain," Frank protested. "I put in four months on the line in combat to get that one stripe."

"That is unfortunate Private. You are dismissed."

Frank turned and left the office. "Bastard. Bastard. Bastard, Bastard, Bastard." Frank mumbled as he walked past Sergeant Riley.

"Agreed," Riley said.

"He busted me for one lousy D.R."

"He gets a kick out of it, the heartless bastard."

Frank hurried down to the formation and marched to class. The first hour was Army Regulations.

"Let's study Article 15, this morning," Frank requested.

They studied Article 15. All day they studied Article 15. On their smoke breaks they studied it, on their lunch hour they studied it. From 0900 until 1700 they studied Article 15. At 1730 Frank reported to the CQ and requested his pass.

"It's not in the box," the CQ reported.

"Hear that fellows, my pass isn't in the box."

"Call the Captain and find out why my pass isn't in the box," Frank demanded.

"OK Frank, but it'll be your funeral if he doesn't like it."

The CQ telephoned the Captain.

"It's not in the box because you can't go into town. Your pass is pulled until further notice. Sorry Frank."

"Sorry hell. Let's go fellows. They say the I.G. is a pretty square shooter, we'll give him a little target practice."

The ten men of the Unfit Outfit marched as a unit to Colonel Fizbee's residence. Frank called the men to attention and saluted smartly when the Colonel answered the door.

Colonel Fizbee was of medium height, an old, old Army man with dark blue eyes and a perpetual smile on his face which was practically covered with his thick, bushy mustache which hung down over the corner of his lips. Despite the smile there was a certain look of sadness and compassion that filled his face.

The Colonel invited the men in and Frank explained the problem.

"Why that's double punishment," Colonel Fizbee remarked after hearing Frank's story.

"That's what we thought Colonel, what can we do about it?"

"Do about it? You can do plenty about it. Those rules weren't written to protect him. I'm going to call Captain Thompson and right away too, damn it. And you're getting your stripe back too, since he didn't comply with Article 15, then the punishment he inflicted isn't technically legal."

The Colonel went into the next room and made a telephone call. "I don't give a damn if you are eating your dinner, Captain, get over to your office and give that man his pass and right away too."

The men snapped to attention and saluted the Colonel. Frank thanked him and the men echoed the thanks.

"Any time boys. That's what an I.G. is for, to see that justice is done. I don't like that damn civilian bastard anyway."

The men marched back to the office and Captain Thompson begrudgingly gave Frank his pass. The following morning the fellows took a new interest in Army Regulations. Why, there was no limit to the possibilities if they would only be dedicated students.

7

Sick Call

Monday morning and 10 men were AWOL. Needless to say, Captain Thompson was more than a little concerned with the morning report. In fact when he got a look at the sick call list, he blew his top. At noon when the men returned from class he called for a special assembly.

"You men are taking advantage of a good thing. Sick Call is for sick people." The Captain paused for a full moment for emphasis and then continued. "We don't want you going on sick call just so that you can miss going to class. From now on I don't want to hear of anyone going on sick call unless he is close to death."

"He plans on putting 'I told you I was sick,' on our grave stones?" Frank lamented.

"He's the guy that is sick. He's sick in the head," Charlie remarked.

That afternoon the men started studying Army Regulations on Sick Call. The next morning studies continued. As the class assembled to return that afternoon Charlie Fenner called Corporal Tuttle aside, "Corporal, I have to go on emergency Sick Call."

"But what will the Captain say?" Tuttle stammered.

"Let him say what he wants to. I have an emergency condition and I have go on emergency Sick Call."

"Me too, Corporal," Frank said.

"We've all got to go," Tom explained.

"Now wait a minute, this is a trick. Now you guys fall in, we're going to class."

"Maybe you are Corporal, but we're all going on emergency Sick Call," Frank said. "What we have won't wait until tomorrow morning. We've got to go right now."

The Unfit Outfit fell in and marched to the dispensary while Corporal Tuttle marched to class alone.

"Now remember fellows, to pull this off we've got to convince that doctor that there is something wrong with us," Frank explained.

"That'll be easy, remember, we're all 'B' profiles. Those damn doctors were the ones that made us 'B' profiles. They've already said we were unfit. It shouldn't be too hard convincing them that there is something wrong," Charlie said, as a new limp appeared in his walk.

"The doctor's still out to lunch, be back about 1400," the dispensary clerk explained.

"No hurry, we're all set to spend the rest of the afternoon in here," Charlie admitted, as he winked at the others.

"I wonder how Tuttle is doing at class?" Frank joked. "He really needs a little private tutoring anyway, he just doesn't seem to take the interest in Army Regulations that we do. No imagination."

Someone brought out a deck of cards and the fellows were deeply engaged in a penny Black Jack game when the doctor finally arrived at 1430.

"What's this?" the doctor asked, as he hung up his jacket and rolled up his sleeves.

"Black Jack," Frank said. "Want in?"

"I haven't been in a good penny Black Jack game in years," the doctor admitted. "Deal me in."

"Sixteen, you want a hit?" Frank asked.

"Sure hit me."

"Busted."

"Damn it!"

"It's only a penny Sir."

"I shouldn't have hit sixteen."

After an hour of hot and heavy playing the Doctor was down seventeen cents.

"Guess it just isn't my day. Say, what in the hell are you fellows doing here anyway?"

"Wounds."

"All of you?"

"Yep. We're all unfit."

"Want me to take a look?"

"Do you have to?"

"Nope," the doctor said.

"It's OK with us then, just so you keep a record."

The doctor made a short note of each man's name and the nature of his wound.

"Now who's deal is it?"

"Yours doc, looks like the last hand, it's almost 1700. Time for chow and then passes."

"Hate to see you fellows go. How about coming back again some day? I sure got a kick out of this game. Say, shouldn't you fellows be in class?"

"Yep, but you see doc, this was an emergency," Frank explained, as he lost another penny to the fast dealing doctor.

"Oh, yeah, that's right, it was, wasn't it?"

The men assembled outside the dispensary and marched back to the barracks. Tuttle was waiting for them.

"How was emergency sick call?" he asked.

"I think it did us all a lot of good," Frank said as he jingled his new won fortune in his pocket.

"Now we'll see what the Captain has to say," Tuttle sneered.

After dinner the men reported to the Orderly Room for passes. Captain Thompson was on hand for the occasion.

"No passes for you fellows. If you're too sick to go to class, then you're too sick to go to town."

"But Captain, those medics did wonders. Fixed up every one of us, just like that," Frank said, snapping his fingers for emphasis.

"No passes," the Captain snapped.

"That final?" Tom asked.

"Final," the Captain said.

The men formed a formation in front of the building and marched to the residence of Colonel Fizbee.

"How are you fellows? Come on in," the Colonel said, swinging the door wide open in a gesture of genuine hospitality.

"What have you got going for you now?"

"Emergency Sick Call," Frank explained. "The Captain pulled our passes for going on Emergency Sick Call."

"What did you go on Emergency Sick Call for?" the Colonel asked.

"Well, you see, Colonel, yesterday Captain Thompson gave us his big speech about not going on sick call. It just didn't seem right, after all, if a man is sick then he should go on sick call and we just didn't go for the way the Captain was handling the matter."

"And so we thought up this deal about emergency Sick Call," Tom explained. "The Doctor fixed us up real good and now we want to go to town but the Captain pulled our passes."

"We think the Captain is wrong," Louis added.

"What did he pull your passes for?" the Colonel asked.

"For going on emergency Sick Call," Tom explained. "He says if we're too sick to go to class then we're too sick to go to town."

"Is Captain Thompson a doctor?"

"Nope." Everyone agreed.

"Then I'm afraid that Captain Thompson has made another serious mistake. Now don't you fellows think that I'm saying you did the right thing going on Emergency Sick Call. What I am saying is that Captain Thompson just isn't going by the regulations and as the Inspector General it's my job to see that everything goes by the book."

The Colonel went into the next room and the men sat silently, listening to the telephone conversation.

"Doctor, this is Colonel Fizbee. I have 10 fellows here and they tell me they had to go on Emergency Sick Call today and they claim you fixed them up. Do you think they are well enough to go to town?" The Colonel paused a minute and then said, "B Profiles?" He paused another minute and said, "Every one of them has a Purple Heart." There was an especially long pause and then the Colonel said, "Unfit for Combat Duty and you got to them just in time? That's nice doctor. It's good to know that we have such an efficient Medical Department on the Post. Thanks Doc."

The Colonel walked slowly into the room where the men were anxiously waiting. He looked very solemn and sat down and remained silent for a whole minute. Then he looked up at the men and asked, "You fellows think that Captain Thompson is pretty chicken shit, don't you?"

"You hit it right on the head," Louis said.

"And you'd like me to put him in his place, wouldn't you?" the Colonel continued.

"Right," the men replied.

"Well I'll be damned if I'll call the Captain on this one. You fellows are just sharp shooting and you won't get my help if I feel that you are just trying to use me to harass the Captain. When he gets out of line and starts kicking the regulations around so that it's downright unfair, then I'm with you 100 percent, but let me warn you, don't go looking for trouble for the Captain like you did this time. He'll get into enough trouble by himself without you setting him up like a duck in a shooting gallery."

"I guess you're right Colonel," Charlie said. He looked a little sad but he knew the Colonel was being a right guy.

"I guess we're getting a little chicken ourselves," Louis said.

"And a night in camp might give us all a little letter writing time," Frank suggested.

"You're a right guy, Colonel," Ben said. "Thanks for keeping us in line."

The Colonel smiled, "That's my job. Keeping everyone in line. Oh, and by the way before I forget," the Colonel winked. "Why don't you men drop over some evening? I haven't had a good penny Black Jack game for a long, long time. Will you do that for me?"

8

Secret Agent

Captain Thompson was a little hesitant to do anything that might affect the Personnel Management Class, or "The Unfit Outfit," as they called themselves. He was wounded, but far from being defeated. He was just biding his time waiting for the men to make a mis-move. He waited one day, two days then a whole week and nothing happened. When he could wait no longer, he sent for Corporal Tuttle. When Corporal Tuttle received the message to report to the Captain, the blood ran from his tiny frame. He adjusted his uniform and then ran all the way to the office.

"Corporal Tuttle reporting as ordered, Sir," Tuttle snapped.

"Ah yes, Corporal Tuttle. At Ease. Sit down Corporal, I want to talk to you about your men."

"I've tried to talk to your Sergeant, Sir, but he doesn't seem concerned."

"Corporal, let me tell you something. Sergeant Riley is a very poor non-commissioned officer. No respect for officers. No sense of leadership. No loyalty to his Commanding Officer. A very, very poor non-commissioned officer."

"That is what I thought, Sir. Why, at Leadership School they taught us to respect authority."

"Oh, you went to Leadership School, Corporal?"

"Yes Sir, and I'm sure having a tough time getting these men to understand that I'm their leader."

"That is what I called you in for, Corporal. As you know they have been acting like a bunch of smart asses. No respect for officers. No discipline. Very poor soldiers. Why, when I was in the Second World War. You knew I saw action in the Second World War, didn't you Corporal?"

"Well Sir."

"Yes, Corporal," the Captain continued. "When I was in the Second World War, well, back then the men had respect for their officers."

"What do you want me to do Captain?" Tuttle asked.

"Just keep your eyes and ears open. Find out what they are up to and let me know. We'll work together Corporal. We'll keep them in line. Whenever you find out something let me know about it. Don't bother going to Sergeant Riley, I want you to report directly to me, understand?"

"Yes Sir, Captain!" Tuttle said as his voice broke from the excitement he felt.

The conversation apparently ended, Tuttle snapped to attention, saluted, did a smart about face and marched out of the office right into Sergeant Riley.

"Corporal, will you please stop marching around my office. Please look where in the hell you're going, OK?"

"I'm sorry, Sir, I mean Sergeant."

Sergeant Riley had overhead the conversation and it left a bad taste in his mouth. He didn't know exactly what to do about it. He was quite sure that the fellows could take care of themselves but just to make sure he decided to tip them off. As Frank walked past the Orderly Room, Riley spotted him and called, "Hey Frank, you got a minute?"

"Sure Sarg, what's up?"

"Well, there's a little plot going on and I thought I might as well let you in on it. It seems that the Captain is a little disturbed about the way you've been teaching him regulations. He called that poor excuse for a Corporal in here a few minutes ago and made a deal with him to spy on you. Just thought you'd like to know."

"Sure thing Sarg. Maybe we can have a little fun with this."

"That is what I was thinking Frank. That is what I was hoping."

The two men slapped each other on the shoulder and parted. Frank immediately called a special meeting of the Unfit Outfit and 10 eager minds went to work on a plot with more enthusiasm and excitement then they'd had in weeks.

"As I see it," Frank reasoned, "we've got to let Tuttle in on some big plan. Let's all kick it around for a few days and see what we can come up with."

The Unfit Outfit bounced around several brilliant ideas. At first they thought of telling Tuttle that they were going to blow up the school. Next, they thought of hinting at assassinating the Captain. They finally agreed on a much less drastic plan.

Little Sammy was the quiet one in the group. He went to town faithfully every night and when he got to town with the boys he always made some excuse and went off by himself. The fellows all suspected that he had a girlfriend that he was keeping to himself, however he wouldn't talk about it. It was decided that Sammy would be the center of attraction in the big plot.

Captain Thompson aided the progress that morning at assembly by making the statement that the men were taking too long making up formation. In the future any man late for the formation would be confined to quarters on his off duty time, for one week. At the next formation, always prompt, never late Sammy, came running into the ranks five minutes late. He was immediately informed that he was restricted to quarters for one week.

The next morning Frank was elected to have a chat with Corporal Tuttle. He took Tuttle over to the corner of the barracks and after making a big show to see that no one else was listening, he approached Tuttle in a low voice.

"I wouldn't let you in on this Corporal, if I didn't think I could trust you."

"Why, you know you can trust me," Tuttle lied.

"Well, you know little Sammy is confined to quarters for a week and we're afraid of what he's going to do. He's been talking about deserting. He's almost out of his mind. You see he's got a little gal in town and the guy is really in love. He's an awful jealous fellow and he's been thinkin' all sorts of weird things about what his gal is doing when he isn't around. We don't want him to desert or get in trouble so we figured out this plan. Since there are a lot of extra cots here, we just figured we could smuggle Sammy's gal into camp and let her stay here with us until Sammy can get his pass back. We can get her chow from the mess hall and once we get her past those M.P.s at the gate we figure we'll have it made. It seems like the least we can do for a buddy."

"Ah, yeah," Tuttle almost acted like he agreed without really doing so as this was the kind of a trick he could report back to the Captain.

"Now, here is our plan and how you fit in. We figure we'll use your uniform since you're so short. Almost the same height as Sammy's girl." Tuttle looked a little offended as Frank continued. "We'll go to town and at 2200 we'll all come back to camp with the gal dressed in your uniform. Why, we shouldn't have a bit of trouble. How about it, can we count on you to supply the uniform?" Frank asked.

"Well, I'd like a little time to think about it. I'll see you later." Tuttle turned and almost broke his leg running to the Captain's office. He was out of breath when he arrived. He saluted, and still panting said, "Ca ha tan, ah ah they're gonna bring in a girl."

"Now slow down," the Captain shouted. "Catch your breath man. What's this all about?"

Tuttle took a deep breath and continued, "You told me to keep my ears open. Well, Captain, they took me in on their plot. They plan to bring Sammy's girl in to live with him while he's restricted to the barracks."

"You're kidding."

"No, I'm not kidding Captain, they want to borrow my uniform. What should I do?"

"Let them have it Corporal. Now let's go over this again. I want to write down a few of the facts."

"Well, Captain, you restricted Sammy to the barracks for being late for formation. He's in love with this Japanese girl in town and he has threatened to desert just to be with her, so the fellows decided that to keep Sammy out of trouble that they would bring his girl to the barracks to live with him."

"But how would they get her on the base?"

"That is where my uniform comes in. They plan to dress her like a G.I. Corporal and let her march in with them tonight."

"That is fine Corporal, just let them try it. I'll get the Provost Marshall and the M.P.s and we'll fix it so that we can Court Martial every one of them."

"Swell, Captain. They plan to bring her through the gate at 2200."

"Just give them the uniform, Corporal, I'll take care of everything else."

Tuttle saluted and ran back down the hall to the men.

"I'll do it!" he shouted excitedly.

The men took turns shaking his hand and patting him on the back.

"Good old Corporal Tuttle," Frank remarked. "I knew we could count on him."

"Guess you're not such a bad guy after all Tuttle," Tom said as he gave Tuttle a hearty handshake.

Tuttle did not reply.

After class the men made a great fuss about relocating the cots. They moved Sammy down to the last cot in the corner and left the cot next to it vacant. Some of the fellows dug into their foot lockers and came up with thin silky things they had purchased in town to take home to their girlfriends. They laid them out neatly on the empty cot. Next a great array of food was stored in an empty foot locker and the final touch was added when one of the men started burning incense. Corporal Tuttle delivered the uniform to Frank who then made a great deal out of finding an overseas cap that was big enough for Sammy's girlfriend to conceal her elaborate hair-do. Everything was ready and the men, with the exception of Corporal Tuttle and Sammy, marched into town. As soon as the men left, Corporal Tuttle made his way to the Captain's office.

"They're on their way Captain. They took my uniform and it's all set. They'll be coming back through the gate at 2200 with the girl."

"I've taken care of everything Corporal. The Provost Marshall, himself, will be standing by the gate. They have ten extra M.P.s standing by. Just let them come throught the gate," Captain Thompson said. "We'll Court Martial every one of them."

The moments ticked by very slowly for Captain Thompson. He didn't mind waiting though. Revenge was so sweet. Let that Inspector General Fizbee try to get the men out of this one.

Finally the moment arrived. Exactly 2200.

The men assembled a block from the gate. Nine men from class and one corporal. The Oriental features of the party in the Corporal's uniform stood out like a sore thumb. The men all checked each other over to see that their uniforms were in proper order. They all held their passes in their hand and took a deep breath. Together they walked to the gate. As they got to the gate an army of M.P.s descended upon them.

"What seems to be the trouble?" Frank asked innocently.

"It looks like your little plot failed," the M.P. said as he motioned for the men to walk into the Provost Marshall's office.

"What did we do?" Tom asked.

"We just want to check you over to see that everything is OK," the M.P. explained.

"Now take off your caps," the Provost Marshall ordered.

The men took off their caps and each one of them wore a look of complete innocence.

"You there Corporal. Let me look at that pass. Mizuho Kobo? What kind of name is that Corporal?"

"It is Japanese, sir. I'm from Hawaii. I'm attending Cook School here."

"That sure looks like a G.I. haircut he has, or she has, or whatever," the Provost Marshall began to stammer. "I don't, I don't, I don't know what in the hell to think. Sergeant, suppose you lock all of these men up for a minute. I want to talk with Captain Thompson." The Provost Marshall was bewildered. He called the Sergeant over in the corner and whispered, "Sergeant, find out if that Corporal is a man or a woman."

"Now Sir, how in the hell can I do that?"

"I don't care how you do it, but find out Sergeant and find out fast."

The Sergeant scratched his head and then shook his head a couple of times as he walked toward the cell where the corporal was waiting.

"Corporal, do you have any other papers on you?"

"Sure Sarg. My I.D. Card. Geneva Convention Card. Civilian Driver's License. Dog tags, pictures. Just what would you like to see?"

"If I told you what I want to see, Corporal, you would think I was a queer."

"What do you mean, Sergeant?" the Corporal asked innocently.

"Oh, to hell with it. Never mind. Maybe the Provost Marshall will talk to you." The sergeant turned and made a speedy exit.

"Sir, the man has proper credentials. He's a Corporal in the United States Army."

"Did you check him Sergeant?"

"Sir, I checked him all I'm going to check him. If you want a closer inspection then I suggest that you do it yourself."

"Wait'll I get ahold of Captain Thompson. He sure botched this up. What in the hell is he trying to pull? Maybe he thinks this is a good joke? Sergeant, get Thompson on the phone." The Sergeant quickly dialed the number and Captain Thompson answered on the first ring.

"Yes sir, this is Captain Thompson, did it work OK?"

"Captain, if this is your idea of a practical joke," the Provost Marshall screamed.

"Joke? What do you mean Joke? Did you get the girl?"

"Captain, there is no girl?"

"No girl?" The Captain was stunned. "But the men took the uniform to town and they laid out silky things on the bed and they---"

"Damn it, Captain, you've gone far enough with this thing. I want you to know that I'm making an official report of the entire incident so you'd better be prepared to defend yourself."

The men were released immediately. The Provost Marshall apologized for the entire matter. The men said they understood, it was just a big mistake. It could happen to anyone. Just forget it, no doubt the Captain was suffering from a nervous condition. They marched to the Beer Hall and laughed themselves silly the rest of the night. When they returned to the barracks, Corporal Tuttle was sitting on his bunk with tears rolling down his cheeks. Sammy was sitting on his cot with a big grin.

"The Captain just came in and said that my restriction was lifted. I could go to town right now if I wanted. He looked awful pale."

"How did it go?" Tuttle asked faintly.

"What go?" Frank asked.

"The girl?" Tuttle asked.

"What girl?" Tom asked innocently.

"Sammy's girl, you know."

"Don't know what in the hell you're talking about, Corporal. Now let's hit the sack, OK? We've got a busy day and we have to study a few more regulations tomorrow. I wonder what the book says about false arrest."

Corporal Tuttle turned whiter yet. "Goodnight," he said weakly.

"Goodnight, good old Corporal Tuttle," Tom replied.

9

Pachinko

The business about the girl in town was all right with Sammy, he went along with the gag as the Unfit Outfit had asked, but he really didn't have a mad affair going in town as they claimed. Oh, he had done a small amount of experimenting when they first hit the Island like any normal G.I. might do, but the fascination soon wore off and he got around to more important things. What could be more important on the Island of Eta Jima than the girls? There was only one answer to that question in Sammy's mind. The most important thing was the machines. Gambling machines. Any kind at all. Slot machines, pinball machines, any kind of machines, just as long as they involved gambling.

At first Sammy watched the play and he saw the joy on the players' faces when the bell rang and the jackpot paid off. Sammy had been watching machines since he was 13. He had spent all of his spare time around the pinball machines in the corner drugstore. In a year he was the champ and could beat any kid in town. Then he had progressed to the back room of the pool hall where one-armed bandits lined the walls. The machines were like a religion to Sammy, he studied them closely and played the slots only when his careful scrutiny told him that a payoff was due. After all, with slots it was all in the percentages. You couldn't just play and win. They were set against you and the only way to make out was to study the machines and make your play when the machine was ready.

When Sammy was drafted he didn't like the situation at all. Like every other G.I. he found the physical activities exhausting and the classes a drag. When they brought out the 30 caliber machine gun Sammy fell in love with it. When he first squeezed the trigger he discovered that the feeling was the same sensation as when he pulled in a jackpot on a slot machine. Every chance he got after that he spent tearing a machine gun apart and learning what made it fire, why it jammed and how to get it back into operation in a hurry. He learned that the rapid firing vibration caused an arousal in his groin that excited him. It was much better than his own M-1 rifle, so when he arrived in Korea he quickly volunteered for a machine gunner's job. It was a tough job, expecially for Sammy, because he was only 5 feet six inches tall and weighed less than 140 pounds.

Whenever the rest of the squad would take a break, Sammy would throw his gun on his back and run with it, crawl with it and then practice setting it up in a hurry. The practice rapidly paid off, as Sammy soon had over twenty Chinese to his credit. It wasn't so bad firing from a bunker but on an attack you had to let loose a whole belt of ammo and move to another position before a mortar or grenade came in on you.

The day Sammy got hit they were attacking a high hill and Sammy was assigned to fire cover for the point platoon. The first group went up the strongly fortified hill. He fired off one belt and the enemy was falling everywhere. He could have moved to a safer position but the fellows needed the support right away and so he threw another belt into his gun and was half through it when the mortar came in and silenced him. He came to in the M.A.S.H. unit and found he had a half a dozen small shrapnel wounds. Nothing serious, a little concussion, not bad enough to keep him from playing the slot machine in the Hospital. Then they sent him to Osaka General Hospital in Japan for his wounds to heal and from there to Eta Jima.

Sammy eyed the Pachinko machines carefully. Pachinko was different from either Pinball or Slots, it was a combination of skill and luck. That first night Sammy had ventured only 50 yen and took his time and played for quite a while before losing. The next night he studied the play a little longer and this time ventured 100 yen. Again he lost but found that he was getting better with every try. For the next week he just studied the machines and worked on the odds. He picked out a couple of steady winners and watched them operate. It was easy to find the winners. With every big win a bell rang and a cheer went out from the crowd. After two weeks Sammy felt more confident and he went at the game full strength. At curfew time he cashed in his balls and returned to camp with a carton of cigarettes. Now the game was really getting to Sammy. He wanted to spend all of his time playing. Each evening after chow he would get his pass and head down Cherry Street to the Pachinko Parlor. Funny but Sammy seemed to be the only G.I. in Japan that was interested in the game. True there were many other items of interest to be found on Cherry Street that might be considered more interesting to a G.I. but to Sammy the girls didn't even run a close second.

Maybe he was getting too familiar with the game and this made him careless but for some reason he hit a miserable losing streak. He was spending more each night and winning nothing. Then one weekend he spent both days at the machines and when he returned to camp on Monday morning he was broke. Instead of the losses discouraging him, they only made him more determined to really lick the machines once and for all.

Going broke was the best thing that could have happened to Sammy. He had time to lay on his cot and dream, ponder and think about all the different ways of hitting those machines right on down the line. With his knowledge of gambling machines he knew there had to be a way of coming back each night with crates of merchandise as his reward. He knew that before leaving Eta Jima he would be victorious, it was only a matter of time. He figured out a system and you couldn't beat a system when it came to gambling machines. As soon as payday rolled around he would be at it again.

10

Memories

"Whatta ya say we call on the old Colonel and have a Black Jack Game tonight?" Tom asked the men as class let out.

"OK by me," Charlie said. "Maybe he can find a way back into infantry duty for us."

"Do you think he might?" they all asked.

"Who knows?" Charlie said. "At least we can try."

After chow the men assembled in front of the hall and marched to the Colonel's home. He came to the door and seeing the men there, he broke out into a big friendly smile. "What is it tonight, men?" he asked.

"Just a social call," Tom explained. "Thought you might be interested in a little Black Jack game."

"Interested?" he said, opening the door wide. "I haven't thought of anything else for the past few days. Come on in and I'll set up the table."

The Colonel had a large beer cooler chucked full and at intervals throughout the evening he restocked it from his adequate supply in the cellar. The game was hot and heavy and finally the men took a break to enjoy a cigarette and beer.

"You live alone here Colonel?" Tom asked.

"Yes, I'm batchin' it. I have a houseboy who cooks and cleans and goes home every night. How about another round of beer fellows?"

"Didn't you ever get married Colonel?" Charlie asked.

"Well not really, that's a long story and you fellows wouldn't be interested," he said.

"Sure we would Colonel, tell us about your love life."

"You sure you'd be interested?"

"Sure," they all replied.

"Well, it was back in 1939," the Colonel began. "I first came to Japan as a First Lieutenant and I had a special assignment in Toyko. I was assigned to the American Embassy there. I'd been there a month when I met Toshiko. She worked in a club and I got pretty well involved with her in a couple of weeks." He paused and took a long drink from his can of beer and then he continued. "After about a month we set up housekeeping and from then on I had the happiest two years of my life. She was wonderful, always trying to make me happy, a perfect wife. Only thing, we never did get around to actually getting married. You know how it is, you keep putting it off and pretty soon a month becomes a year and then two years. I had planned to stay in the Army anyway and there was no reason why I couldn't just keep on living in Japan on the same assignment, so I never got around to marriage." He paused and said, "Get me another beer Louie." Then he continued, "Well, then about the last week of November, 1941, we got our orders to leave Japan immediately. Had only about eighteen hours notice. All I could do was kiss her goodbye and leave. A week later comes Pearl Harbor and I was assigned to Washington, D.C. for the whole war. After V-J Day I pulled a few strings and got assigned to the Occupation Forces. I spoke Japanese pretty well and after a few months I got an assignment in Tokyo. Then I spent two years in Tokyo looking for Toshiko. Finally I ran into a friend of hers and she remembered that about six months after I left, Toshiko started dating a Japanese Naval Officer. She wrote down his name for me. Seems that he had been transferred here to Eta Jima for training and she'd followed him. Apparently they had a place in Hiroshima and he'd been assigned to the submarine base here. It took nearly a year but I finally got a transfer here to Eta Jima."

The men were sitting silently taking in every word.

"Did you find her?" Charlie asked.

"Well, I was able to determine that the sailor was killed in action about a year before V-J day. Then I got a few more leads and I'm pretty sure that Toshiko was in Hiroshima when the bomb dropped."

"Was she listed as a casualty?" Louis asked.

"No, but the casualty list was pretty useless. There were hundreds that were never found or identified. Every weekend I go to Hiroshima to look for her. Almost four years now I've been looking."

"Ever try the newspapers or a detective agency?" Sammy asked.

"No. It's funny fellows, I'm not really sure that I want to find her. It's good duty here at Eta Jima. Not too much work, beautiful climate, I love the Japanese people and I have several lady friends. Finding Toshiko is just my goal in life. Everyone should have some kind of an goal. You don't have to reach that goal, in fact I guess if I found her I'd be pretty miserable because I'd have lost my goal. When I found out she'd taken off with that Japanese fellow I was pretty badly broken up. I still look for her, but somehow I'm afraid that I might really find her. Maybe I'm not really looking for her at all. Maybe I'm just looking for the youth I had when I was with her. I guess I'm talking kind of silly, maybe it's the beer, anyway I've talked enough, how about a few more hands?"

"You're not talking silly Colonel," Charlie said. "I think we all know what you mean by a goal. Take us for instance. We've all got a goal to get back in the Infantry. Now that may seem pretty silly, after all, being in the Infantry is a hell of a rough life. In combat you don't get enough chow, no beer. You practically go without any sleep and your living with the thought that any second a mortar or an artillery round might come in with your name on it. You're dirty all the time, cold at night, bitchin' every minute of it. Just one thing. You're a man. A whole man, doin' a man's job. Sort of like a gladiator in the old times. You can hold your head high. You better be careful where you hold it high or you might get it blown off, but anyway you've a right to hold it high. Now the Army says we'll make good clerks. Hell, that's like castrating a bull. Imagine how a bull must feel. Yes Sir, Colonel, we've got a goal."

"That's right," Ben agreed. "Can you help us Colonel?" he asked.

"Not if the medics say you are 'B' Profiles, Unfit for Combat Duty," the Colonel explained. "I wish I could but there is nothing I can do for you."

"Aw, what in the hell do you say we get back to the game?" Louie barked.

"Sure, get us another round of beer and I'll deal," the Colonel agreed.

And so it went, another deal, another beer. When the evening was finished the men had consumed a grand total of eight full cases of beer and a fifth that the Colonel had thrown in as a nightcap. As the men slowly bid the Colonel goodnight he saluted smartly and shook each man's hand.

"And come back again fellows," he called as they headed slowly back to the barracks.

"Any time Colonel," they answered. "Any time."

It was 0200 when the men finally got out on the road for the march back to the barracks. They were feeling no pain. In fact, they were feeling nothing. They had stumbled along together less than a block when they came to a sign that told them they were passing

Captain Thompson's quarters.

"We ought to take a garbage can and put it up against his front door," Louie suggested.

"Why not?" Charlie agreed. "Looks like he's asleep. There are no lights on."

"Then when he opens the door in the morning, WHAMMO, garbage all over the floor."

"Let's get that garbage can over there and do it," Frank said, grabbing ahold of the can. "Hell, it's empty, an empty garbage can wouldn't be any good."

"Why don't we fill it with something?" Charlie suggested.

"Ya," Louis agreed. "I got to take a leak anyway."

"So do I," Frenchie said.

"What if we get caught?" Ben asked.

"Screw it!" Frenchie said. "I figure we've got just four more weeks to fuck up bad enough to get kicked out of this clerk's school. We better start right now."

"Yeah, sit the can down and we'll fill it up," Tom said. Tom had consumed the greater share of beer and was the most willing to contribute.

Perhaps a passer by would have thought the 10 men were gathered around a campfire singing college songs. Maybe they gave the appearance of a football team huddled together before the big play of the game. In a few moments the huddle was broken and four of the men struggled with the now heavy can. Carefully they set it against the Captain's door at just the right angle. This ritual completed the men marched quietly back to the barracks and retired.

They had just about gone to sleep when Tom went into a drunken laughing spell. The laughter was soft at first but it gradually built into a roar.

"What's so funny?" Louis asked.

Tom struggled to stop laughing long enough to answer. "I was just wondering," he said thickly. "If that S.O.B. can swim."

The following morning Captain Thompson awoke with a cheery disposition. He carefully wiped the dust off his shoes and, after giving his silver bars a final shine, he headed for the door anticipating a fine breakfast at the Officer's Mess. Before turning the door knob, he stood erect assuming the correct posture for an officer. Shoulders back, chest out, chin in, head held high. In a precise military manner he turned the door knob and swung the door wide open. With a loud thud the can came flying in, narrowly missing the Captain's leg as it sailed through the doorway. With a sudden splash the Captain was transformed into a soaking, raging mess. "Those men," he screamed. "Those rotten fuckin' bastards. They've done this to me and they'll pay for it." The Captain slipped to the slick floor. He made a fist and pounded it on the wet puddle around him. "They'll pay for this!" he screamed. "Every one of them will pay in full."

11

Housekeeping

Charlie Fenner had a steady girl back home. She was 17 years old and a senior in high school. Not that Charlie thought much of the idea of going steady. He never could understand it, but it was the code of the times. Everyone went steady. He'd have much preferred to take out a variety of girls, but everyone went steady and it was so darn important to her that he finally gave Janet his high school ring and listened to her talk of loving him forever as he left for overseas. He was careful not to say anything to her that he did not really mean and so he had said very little. When she wrote and wanted to go to "just the Christmas dance" with another fellow, he was more than willing to let her. Then the New Year's date was OK'd and he began feeling silly being asked like that, when he was really hoping she'd just drop that silly "steady" business and go out and date fellows like a girl her age should. It was a real relief when he received that "Dear John" letter saying she was deeply interested in someone else and felt obligated to call off their "going steady." He felt freed from an entanglement that was not his doing or his desire.

Now he was truly a free man. That night he dressed very carefully and headed for town. He hadn't paid much attention to the girls before this. He did observe that the Oriental women looked less and less Oriental every day. It was getting so that they looked good to him, mighty damn good. Up until now he had just brushed off their propositions without even thinking about them. They were somehow out of the question until now. Now things were a little different. Not that he approved of paying a gal for her affection. He'd done it once in the States and after it was over he felt dirty and miserable. Of course the fellows all said it was different with these young Japanese girls. Anyway, he just thought he'd go to town and walk around and see what was going on and everything. He walked slowly down Cherry Street and for the first time he actually realized that these girls were all available. Why, there must have been at least three, maybe four hundred girls and they were all for the taking. All young, soft, tender, sweet smelling and sexy, in a different way than he had ever notice before. They were available but they weren't cheap about it. They made it seem like an enjoyable legitimate profession. These girls weren't hopeless alcoholics who had lost a love, nor were they narcotic bugs willing to do anything to support their habit. These were nice young gals who were brought up thinking that there purpose in life was to make men happy and they sure looked like they could do a good job. Charlie still wasn't sold. Several offers he received were really tempting, but he just kept on walking. One girl in particular caught his eye. She wasn't very aggressive, in fact she stood back in a dark corner as if she was hoping that none of the passing G.I.s would notice her. Charlie spotted her and walked over and said, "It's a nice night isn't it?"

She smiled and timidly asked, "You comon my house?"

"No not tonight," Charlie replied.

She gave a soft sigh of relief and Charlie noticed it and asked, "Don't you want me to come to your house?"

"It not that G.I. I just don't know you and I don't think I should be out here like this. My G.I. went Stateside last week. Two years I live with him and last month he go home. I no have job, no have money, I don't know what to do, so my girlfriend take me to Mamasan and she think I made good shorttime girl. I scared. You come my house G.I.?"

"What's your name?"

"My G.I. who go home call me Happy. He say I Happy all the time. I no happy right now but you call me Happy, all right G.I.?"

"Sure I'll call you Happy and you call me Charlie."

"Cholly. That's a nice name, Cholly."

Charlie gave Happy a kiss on the cheek and rushed right back to the camp. He took a cold shower and went to bed. He layed there and tossed and turned and kept thinking about Happy. Then he thought about the "Dear John" letter and he thought about his exgirl back home. Why, he'd gone with her for two and a half years and never touched her. Now, here was Happy and the first thing she said to him was "You comon my house." She didn't even say "hello." Just "Let's go to bed." Why, that was a hellava note. And yet she didn't seem cheap, she seemed damned nice. He liked her a lot and it was all he could do to keep from taking her up on her offer. "This sure is a different world over here," he thought. Well, as they say, "When in Rome do as the Romans do." He tossed and turned over a few more times. He started thinking about the other fellows. Weren't they all having a good time with the women? You're damn right they were. But still they were paying for it, and it didn't seem right. He wanted more than a quick lay. Maybe he'd find it. He was sure going to look anyway.

The next evening Charlie was back in town. Again he walked slowly down Cherry Street. Again he was approached by many, many cute young things. Again he walked along wondering where he could find a girl like the one back home. One that he could neck with and take to a movie and talk with about his problems. He had nearly reached the end of the street when he saw her standing in a shadow.

"Hello Cholly," she said softly. "It's a nice evening."

"Ah yah, it is isn't it, Happy."

"Where you go Cholly?"

"Just walkin' around. I don't know. Just lookin' around I guess."

"Were you lookin' for me Cholly?"

"I don't know, I guess I was but I don't really know."

"You want to come to my house Cholly?"

"Sure, I mean no. I mean I don't just want to go to your house to go to bed and that is it."

"What you want Cholly?"

"Well, couldn't we go somewhere and have a beer or something?"

"I'm sorry Cholly, I got no time for that. I business girl and I have to stay here and try to catch G.I."

"How much do you charge?" Charlie gulped, the words stuck in his throat.

"Three Hundred Yen, short time. Fifteen Hundred Yen, all night."

"How much did that other guy you lived with pay you?"

"He no pay, Cholly, he just buy food and pay for room. Maybe, sometimes, he buy me present from P.X., like dress or shoes or somesing nice. You want that same way Cholly? It make me velly happy. I no like short-time business, but I no find job, no have money. I be your girl Cholly. No butterfly. Just your girl Cholly. I cook for you, I wash your clothes, we be velly happy Cholly."

Charlie appeared to be in deep thought. After a full minute he asked her, "How much for the room?"

"One monse eight thousand Yen," she said hopefully.

"And the food?" he asked.

"I won't eat much Cholly, maybe two or three thousand Yen."

"That's about thirty-five bucks. I've just got one more month of school here."

"If you want, I go whereever you go Cholly."

"You'd be true? No other fellows? Just my girl?"

"Just yours Cholly. You want me find a room?"

"Let me think about it. I'll come back and see you tomorrow night."

Charlie turned and walked away. He went into a cabaret and had a beer. Twenty minutes later he was on his way back to camp. He turned to wave to Happy and he saw that she was talking to another G.I. He stood and watched as she took the G.I. by the arm and they walked towards a dark alley together. The blood rushed to his face and felt angry all over. He walked directly to the barracks and went to bed.

Charlie hadn't heard a thing that went on at class that day. He had a lot on his mind. Should he get tied up with a girl that any G.I. in camp could lay for 300 yen? And what if he did get tied with her? Just how true could she be? And what about all the venereal disease that the Army kept saying these women had? Wouldn't it be hell if he caught something? He made up his mind. No sale. He'd go to town and tell her. He dressed very slowly that evening and then, finally, he headed for town.

He needed a haircut anyway, and to tell the truth, he rather dreaded seeing Happy and telling her it was no sale. A Japanese Barber shop was located near the gate on Cherry Street and so Charlie walked into the establishment. An elderly man greeted him with low bows and ushered Charlie to a chair.

"Just a trim," Charlie ordered.

"Hai--Hai, Jo Toe," the man agreed bowing even lower and motioning for the women in the shop to begin.

Immediately one of the elderly women started cutting Charlie's hair. She was just getting good when another of the ladies began shining Charlie's boots. Another women took Charlie's hand and began a manicure. A short time later Charlie was ushered over to a bowl where his hair was washed and then he underwent a vigorous massage. A light oil was then rubbed into his hair, his eyebrows and eyelashed were trimmed, then the hair in his nose and ears was administered to. Then the girls shaved him and applied facial cream to his cheeks and forehead. Next one of them used a small suction cup device to open the pores of his skin. Then hot towels and more hot towels. Another good neck massage and after being thoroughly brushed off Charlie asked for the bad news.

"One Hundred Yen," the man advised.

"One Hundred?" Charlie asked. That was just over 25 cents and Charlie had undergone a complete overhaul.

"One Hundred Yen," the man repeated and Charlie quickly paid the man before he changed his mind.

Charlie left the shop and headed down Cherry Street. Happy was waiting at the end of the street. She saw him approaching and looked very happy.

"Cholly you came like you say."

"Yah Happy, I came but just to tell you it's no deal. I'm just not the guy for you."

Happy was anything but happy. She burst into tears and sobbed.

"But I hoped so that you be mine. I quit job last night, Cholly. I take G.I. to house but no can be that way, so I tell Mamasan I quit."

"You mean you didn't, I mean that fellow didn't."

"I no make short-time girl. I no can go bed with G.I. I don't know or don't love. Only with you Cholly. But now you don't want Happy."

"Stop crying," he said. "Of course I want Happy, I mean, well damn it, we'll do it. Let's go get a room right now."

"Oh Cholly," she cried as she threw her arms around his neck. "I make you good wife Cholly, you see. I cook, I sew, I wash, I make you velly good wife."

Charlie froze. "Wife?" he asked.

"Don't you worry now, Cholly. Just-for-now wife. No wedding. No strings. Just-for-now wife. You get tired of Happy and you say so and that's that. All right?"

"It's a deal. I'll pay for the room and the food and you're my girl. Let's go find a room."

"I got already Cholly. Only six thousand yen a monse. I clean all day hoping you take me. Come on Cholly we go our house."

They walked together, arm in arm. When they reached their room Charlie took off his shoes and went inside. It was spotless. Bamboo walls and floor. A Japanese bed lay rolled up in the corner of the room. There was a charcoal pot in the center of the room and Happy had already prepared their meal. Charlie sat down on the floor and crossed his legs. Happy went outside for a minute and returned with a wide smile on her face.

"I buy you present Cholly. I spend my last 200 Yen for you."

"A jug of beer," Charlie laughed. "Boy this is really a honeymoon Happy, a real honeymoon."

"Somesing else Cholly. Just so you know, I go to Army Dispensary today."

"I'll be damned, Happy, you got a Health Card."
"No V.D. Now you no worry Cholly."
"Now I no worry Happy. Come on over here. I haven't even kissed you yet and we've been just-for-now married for almost an hour."

Happy was velly, velly happy. Cholly was velly, velly happy too. Charlie drank his beer but somehow they never did get around to eating dinner that night. There just wasn't any time to eat and still get back to camp on time.

12

American Made

Corporal Tuttle stayed pretty close to camp. He was a "cherry boy," a virgin. This wasn't of his own choosing, he just never ran into a girl who would say more than, "hello," or "goodbye," mostly the latter. Now that he was in Japan things were a little different, but not much. Sure there were plenty of women available but he was certain that every Japanese female was infected with a terrible, incurable, highly contagious case of syphilis. This he knew from attending Army lectures. He knew how syphilis could make you blind or make you rot away until your private parts fell off. He thought of this every time he looked at a Japanese girl. Whenever one of the girls would approach him on the street he would break into a cold sweat and commence running in the other direction.

Tuttle wasn't much of a drinker either. He'd have a bottle of beer once in a while, but one was his limit. Come to think of it, Tuttle wasn't much of anything. He didn't have any vices but he didn't have any virtues either. He was just sort of blah.

One Saturday evening he had finished his washing and ironing, and he had done a nifty job of cleaning up around his cot, when he decided to take a walk into town. In the interest of health preservation he ran full speed down Cherry Street and into Number One Beer Hall that was located at the far corner of the village. He ordered a beer and sat sipping it when three American women who worked as Army Civilian personnel, came in and took seats at a table nearby. It was obvious that they had been drinking for some time and they were on the make. They weren't doing too well with the G.I.s. Somehow these three overweight, unglamorous creatures in slacks just didn't seem to appeal to the G.I.s who could get all the soft young things they wanted for the price of a beer. One of the women, a brunett who was pushing 30 and 180 at the same time, spotted Tuttle sitting alone and tried to catch his eye.

"Say Corporal, Honey, how would you like to buy me a beer?"

"Tuttle welcomed the thought of talking to a female that wasn't stamped by the Army as suffering from the syphlitic plague.

"Sure maam, I'll be glad to buy you a beer."

Big MaaMoo, as she was known by others, left her girlfriends and took a seat with Tuttle. The fact that she was a good six inches taller and outweighed him by at least 40 pounds didn't seem to bother him at all. He called the waitress over and ordered her a beer and another for himself. By the time he finished his second quart of Asahi beer, nothing seemed to matter. He ordered a third and by then they had transferred from the table to a booth in the corner where Tuttle's chastity was being very much endangered.

"How would you like to have some real fun?" she asked him. "We could get a room and spend the night."

By now Tuttle was game for anything. He'd signed out for an overnight pass anyway, he didn't really expect to use it but they were available for the asking and so he had taken one. They finished their third beer and by now Tuttle was having trouble ambulating. They quickly found a room nearby and it was there that Tuttle spent his first sleepless night with a girl.

When he returned to camp the next morning he was exhausted. He had learned a great deal. She had taught him quite a lot in that first hour, after all, he had a lot to learn. She had tried to continue with a little refresher courses throughout the night. He was happy to get back to camp that morning to get a little rest. Corporal Tuttle slept all day Sunday and right through the night. When he reported to class on Monday he had a guilty worried look on his face as he wondered if the men could tell by looking at him what had happened.

He stayed away from the other men, which was nothing new, usually the other men stayed away from him and the result was the same.

On Tuesday he looked a little more worried. He couldn't seem to keep his mind on the class. Finally, on Wednesday night, he got Louie off into a corner and asked him, "Louie, you've been around. What's it like when you get V.D.?"

"Never had it," Louie said.

"I mean what are the symptoms?"

"An itch, a sore or a drip."

"A drip?"

"That's right. Why?"

"Sh, never mind. I just wondered." Tuttle looked worried.

So worried that the rest of the men took one look at him and they knew what was on his mind. Frank Tucker saw what was going on and gathered a few of his buddies around and after a five minute huddle they went over to where Tuttle was sitting on his sack and seranaded him. They all bowed in Japanese fashion and sang, "Com-on a my house, my house, I'm gonna give you vi-do-ki (V.D.).

Comon a my house, my house,
I'm gonna give you syph and a clap and a gonorrhea too
Ooooo."

Tuttle looked pale, very very pale. He turned away from the fellows and pretended to go to sleep. He only pretended, he didn't sleep at all that night. The next morning he went on sick call. He felt horrible and ashamed. Why him? He'd never even looked at one of those Japanese girls and what happens? He gets something from an American gal.

Tuttle had worked his way to the front of the line at the Dispensary four times and each time he had lost his nerve and gone back to the rear of the line. Now the line was gone and he was their last customer.

"What's the trouble, Corporal?" a medic asked.

"A drip," Tuttle whispered.

The medic gave the usual order that is so familiar to ex-servicemen of all ages. A number of tests were made and for several hours Tuttle sat and suffered in silence. Finally the results of the tests were in and a Medical Captain called Tuttle into his office.

Tuttle could picture his Corporal stripes going down the drain. He slowly saluted and then calling on all his nerve he asked, "What is it Captain?"

The Captain smiled and waited a moment.

"Will I be going blind?" Tuttle asked anxiously. "Will you have to amputate, what is it?"

The doctor laughed. "Just a strain, Corporal. For God's sake take it easy, there's plenty in this Country to go around, you don't have to get it all in one night."

Tuttle turned as red as a beet. He was ashamed and yet he was awfully happy that he wasn't going to go blind or lose his vitals.

"Just take it easy with those women for a few days and you'll be as good as new."

Tuttle saluted and then ran all the way to class. No more American women for him. He guessed he'd just have to be a monk or something.

13

The Bath

Frenchie was sold on all things Japanese. His brief excursions to Nara, Gifu and Nagoya had only whetted his appetite for seeing more of Japan. It was Friday night and he had obtained a two day pass. Such passes weren't the hardest thing in the world to come by because, actually, nothing important happened on the weekend. He looked around the barracks wondering if anyone might be interested in joining him on this cultural excursion.

"The boat ride to Hiroshima is only 300 yen each way," Frenchie explained to Frank Tucker.

"Then it's not for me," he replied. "For 600 yen I can get laid two times right here at Eta Jima."

"Maybe you can," Frenchie argued. "But just think of it, here you are just 300 yen away from one of the most famous cities in the world."

"That's not for this kid," Frank said. "What I want they got right here in town and plenty of it."

Frenchie walked over to Sammy. "What about you Sammy, like to take a weekend pass to Hiroshima with me? I figure we can get by for about twenty bucks."

"Yer kiddin'," Sammy said. "The Pachinko machines are great here, what do you want to go way over there for?"

"You can see where they dropped the Atom Bomb and there are some famous Shrines and..."

"Not for me," Sammy said. "I like the action right here on the Island."

Tom also declined, saying "I can get as drunk as I want to right here on Eta Jima."

Ben was sitting on his cot writing and he overheard the conversation. As Frenchie started towards him he shook his head, "Not for me either, Frenchie, I couldn't afford it. I'd like to go but I just haven't got the money."

Frenchie sounded out the remainder of the group but it was the same story. Either they didn't have the money or else they were satisfied with the bountiful supply right there at Eta Jima. He shined up his brass and his shoes and hit the sack early. He wanted to catch the boat right after breakfast in the morning.

Saturday was another beautiful Spring morning on Eta Jima. Nearly every morning brought sunshine and warmth but this day was especially nice. The sea was calm and every living plant and flower seemed to be in a hurry to grow tall and strong. Frenchie signed out at the office and headed straight for the steamer dock. Cherry Street was just coming alive. The girls were out wandering about, getting ready for a busy Saturday's business. The merchants were setting out their displays. The cabarets were still closed but their doors were wide open, the proprietors hoping to catch a little of the fresh morning air to replace the night's accumulation of stale beer and cigarette odors.

Frenchie made the half mile jaunt to the steamer dock in record time. The boat was already half filled with a wide assortment of Japanese passengers. Old women carrying what might be their sole possessions tied together in large colorful scarfs, business men giving the appearance that they might be commuting to work, a G.I. seated in the corner with his Japanese wife and holding their small daughter.

The loud steam engine started pounding, the whistle blew several times and then they were off. As the boat pulled further away from Eta Jima, Frenchie noticed how mountainous the island really was, hilly, green and beautiful. Frenchie watched the water and it reminded him of his boat ride to Korea months before. Inchon had looked so quiet and peaceful to him and yet just two days later he was in the heavy fighting. Strange how war could make the most peaceful spot in the world into a nightmare.

Soon they were nearing Hiroshima. The long white cement docks were a reminder that this had been a principle Japanese submarine base during the war. Hiroshima had been many things, a great military establishment where detailed plans had been made for the defense of Japan down to the last man. Kamikaze aircraft, suicide boats and swimmers trained to carry huge charges of dynamite, had been in readiness. Near the city, troops had dug in, prepared for what might come. Defense plants worked at full capacity on the morning of August 6, 1945, and the American bomber, Mr. B., dropped a single bomb. Soldiers and women and children died. The bomb did not choose its victims, it killed war mongers and peace lovers alike. It was quick and deadly effective. Nine days later the war ended. The bomb had done its job well. The invasion of Japan by American troops had been avoided.

The people of Hiroshima rebuilt their homes and stores. They buried their dead and healed their sick and wounded. Most of the people held little resentment toward the Americans for dropping the bomb. The Japanese people express their feelings with "Shikata ga nai." Meaning "Oh well, too bad, it is war, and war is a very bad thing."

Frenchie had read that certain things had been set aside in Hiroshima so that all humankind might remember the terrible destruction the bomb had wrought. He got off the boat when it docked and started walking. First, he noticed the wide streets in Hiroshima. Actually they had been put into use before the bomb had dropped. They were a preparation for the bombings, fire lanes to prevent the whole city from burning if the B-29s made a fire bomb raid such as they had been making on Tokyo and other large cities. Other than the wide streets he saw no signs of destruction. Finally he hailed a rickshaw driver and asked him to take him to the Atom Bomb. The driver did not speak English but every rickshaw man knew the meaning of Atom Bomb. It was a short ride and Frenchie was impressed by the beauty and modernism of the Peace Museum. Nearby he saw the Peace Memorial Park. The Memorial Cenotaph in the park contained a stone box which held the known names of 240,000 people who were killed, or who died as a result of the first atomic bomb.

Frenchie saw the Peace Memorial Cathedral and tower, the Memorial Pillar and the huge grave mound of the unidentified victims killed. The area was filled with happy, playing children. Slowly Frenchie toured the Museum. The scream of an air-raid siren down the hall made him remember the war movies. Then an organ played softly and then louder and louder. A scientific display took Frenchie from the caveman days right through Ben Franklin to the Atom Bomb. Vivid photography showed all of the terrible details of destruction. Wrist watches on display documented the time of the blast at 8:16 p.m. Photos showed the ruins of the Shima Hospital, evidence of the great fire, twisted bicycles, melted bottles, then photos of the dead and wounded. Children and mothers burned, scarred, with torn bodies, evidence of the effect of radiation. Horror upon horror, documented in an objective way for the world to remember.

At the rear of the Museum were four impressive views, the first,

Hiroshima before the blast, second the bombing with mushroom clouds and fires, third, the Atomic Desert after the blast, a scene of tragic ruin and then finally Hiroshima Rising, a city rebuilding.

Frenchie left the exhibit with a lump in his throat. His eyes were moist. For an instant he felt ashamed that America had caused so much sorrow and suffering and then he remembered Pearl Harbor. He remembered that this was the price of a victory. He thought of his brother who had died on Battan. He reflected that if the war had lasted another year he'd have been in it. Maybe he'd have been in the invasion of Japan, maybe he too would have died. The Japanese people had the right attitude when they talked about the Americans dropping the bomb. War is war. It is too bad but it is war.

It had been an exhausting day at the exhibits. Frenchie felt tired and sticky. He picked out a clean looking hotel and after quite a linguistic battle he managed to determine that a room for the night ran 500 yen. Use of the bath went with the room. After checking out the room, Frenchie undressed, put on the clogs and Japanese Robe the hotel clerk had loaned him, and headed for the bath. He was in luck. The huge bathroom was empty. It was really three rooms in one; the front room was for dressing, the second for soaping and rinsing. It was filled with steam. The third room was a huge, deep, bath tub. Frenchie quickly soaped and rinsed using a wooden bowl. Then after a gradual process of adapting his body to the temperature of the steaming water he eased himself into the tub. What a glorious feeling. "First bath in seven, no eight, no it's been nine months since I had a bath," Frenchie said half aloud to himself. The Army provided showers most places, but never a bathtub.

Frenchie had been in the tub maybe 15 minutes feeling wonderful when the outer door opened and in walked a girl. And what a girl. Frenchie held his breath hoping she wouldn't notice him but she looked straight at him and smiled as she casually dropped her colorful robe to her feet. She stood proud and erect and her firm round breasts made Frenchie swallow hard. She walked quite gracefully into the steam room and soaped her body throughly. "About eighteen," he guessed, his eyes were glued to her every move. Now she came to the edge of the pool just a few feet from Frenchie and silently slid into the water.

"Hello there," Frenchie said nervously, the words barely clearing his throat.

She blushed now and turned her head away. The water was shoulder deep on her and Frenchie was gathering nerve to reach for her hand when he heard the door. It was an old gray haired man, wearing a thick mustache and a long white goatee. The girl smiled and spoke in rapid Japanese. The only thing Frenchie could decode was "Papasan."

The old man smiled at his charming daughter and then cast a suspicious eye on Frenchie. Frenchie moved a little farther away and assumed a look of complete innocence. The man quickly soaped and rinsed and then joined them in the huge tub. Frenchie climbed from the tub, put on his robe and tongs and headed back to his room. As he left the bath the girl smiled and the old man shook his head and murmured something about all G.I.s The girl hid her laughter politely behind her hand.

The bath had done Frenchie a lot of good. Not only did he enjoy the scenery but the hot steaming water had suddenly relaxed him. Now he was hungry. He suddenly remembered that he had forgotten all about lunch. He would make up for it with a big dinner. Hiroshima's oyster fisheries were world famous. Frenchie decided on a sea food dinner. Somewhere he had read about the Japanese Tempura Bars and with a little searching found one. Tempura is a Japanese dish that is cooked before your eyes. It consists of sea food and vegetables dipped in batter and fried in deep fat. He sat at a counter somewhat like an American Hamburger stand. With the Tempura he received a huge bowl of rice and a pot of tea. "Sake?" the waitress asked. "Hot Sake," he replied, then remembering something else he had read he added, "Hiroshima Sake." The girl smiled and in a moment she returned with a steaming vase of sake together with a small sipping cup. Frenchie dug right in and cleaned up the whole meal. Then after another vase of sake he topped the whole thing off with some Japanese pastry.

Now he felt both clean and well fed. He was ready for a look at Hiroshima at night. He doubled back by the hotel and was about to walk on when he spotted her coming out of the Hotel. At first he didn't recognize her, not with clothes on and all. She was alone and she was very beautiful, the girl in the bathtub. When she spotted Frenchie she smiled modestly and waited for him to speak.

"Where is Papasan?" he asked, looking into the hotel and half expecting him to make an appearance any second.

"Papasan go to Gifu," she replied. "He come back late tomorrow."

"Could I buy you a beer or a sake or something?" he asked, bobbing from one foot to the other and feeling quite self-conscious standing there.

"Papasan tell me stay away from G.I. He say 'Emison, G.I. no good, you stay way from G.I."

"And what do you think?" he asked.

"I don't know G.I. I no afraid of you but maybe Papasan right. Papasan very smart man."

"What else does your father say about G.I.s? Hey, instead of just standing here in the street, let me buy you a cup of tea and you can tell me more about your father."

He took her arm and although she hadn't really decided, he tugged a little and she went along with him. He found a quiet tea house and after removing his shoes they went inside and found a low table in the corner. At his request she ordered the tea and when the girl had served them he offered his cup in a toast and said, "Now let us drink our tea while you tell me about your father's opinion of G.I.s."

"Maybe not very nice, but he say G.I. is 8th evil in this world. Before we have just 7 evils. Earthquake, flood, fire, devils, war, robbery and sickness. Papasan say American G.I. number eight."

"Why so bad?" Frenchie asked.

"Papasan say G.I. drunk all the time and want to go to bed with Japanese girl. You all time get drunk and do this?" she asked.

"Well I don't know, are you giving me an invitation?"

"You make fun of Emison. Maybe Papasan right."

"Now wait Emison, don't get angry, not all G.I.s are like your Papasan says. After all, all the Japanese girls want to get the G.I.s into bed, from what I've seen."

Emison's face got very red and she spoke a little loudly, "That not true. Japanese girls very, very good. Emison not want get you in bed. Emison very nice girl. Maybe Papasan right, G.I. no good."

"Now wait a minute," Frenchie said. "Most G.I.s are about like the company you're with."

"I no understand," Emison said, a puzzled look filled her face.

"What I mean is, if a G.I. is with a nice girl then he's nice. If he's with the other kind, then, well, he just goes along with it."

"You mean if you with nice girl then you be nice?"

"That's right."

"I don't sink so. I sink I better stay away, G.I."

"Now don't go away. I'm harmless. Besides I want you to show me Hiroshima tonight."

"Oh," she said smiling ever so sweetly. "I cannot show you, I not know Hiroshima myself. My house in Sapparo, many miles away. I just visit Hiroshima first time."

"Then we look around together," he suggested.

"I don't know. Papasan get very mad, he find out."
"We won't tell him."
"Well, I want very much see Hijiyama. That big hill just outside city. Go up hill and see all of Hiroshima. See all bright lights and water and everysing."
"Then that's where we'll go," he said, patting her hand.
"I don't sink I should. Maybe all G.I. very bad."
"I promise I'll be good."
"Honto?" she asked.
"What do you mean, honto?"
"Honto, very sacred Japanese promise. I show you." She took Frenchie's right little finger and locked it with her own. "Now you say Honto and no can break promise. Very bad thing if you break Honto promise."
"OK, Honto," he said. "Honto I'll be good."
She smiled. "I believe you keep promise."
They hired a cab and in half an hour they were at the top of the city. A quaint teahouse stood right at the top of the hill and a beautiful miniature Japanese garden adjoined the back terrace. They ordered more tea and sat silently gazing at the fantastic panorama. Frenchie was so moved by the beauty of the scene and Emison that he reached over to hold her hand. She looked offended and quickly took her hands out of reach. "You promise no hanky panky."
"I was just going to hold your hand."
"Never mind, G.I. Papasan say first G.I. take your hand then he take everysing else."
"I wasn't," he stammered. "I wouldn't, I didn't. Oh, to hell with your Papasan. I gave you my word and I'll keep it."
She looked a little unbelieving but there was loving forgiveness in her eyes. "Very beautiful site from Hijiyama, you sink so?"
"I think so," he said, looking not at the site but straight into her warm eyes. "I think you are a very beautiful sight."
She blushed and started to cover her face with her hands but then she stopped and looked at Frenchie. "I sink we better go hotel now. Tomorrow I catch early boat to Miyajima. Better catch early sleep."
"You're going to Miyajima?" Frenchie asked. "So am I. Can we go together?"
"Papasan get very angry he find out."
"We won't tell him," Frenchie said.
"I cannot keep you off boat, if you happen catch same boat, not my fault. Boat leave seven thirty," she said shyly.
"And I'll be on it," Frenchie said. This time he caught her hand

and held it in his squeezing it very gently. She smiled tenderly at Frenchie and said softly, "I think we better go now."

A cab was at the teahouse and the ride down the hill went much faster. When they arrived at the hotel, Emison went in first and asked Frenchie to wait a few minutes. "Hotel man might say somesing to Papasan."

The next morning Frenchie met Emison in the lobby. She did not speak but nodded for him to go out on the street. He went out and waited for her.

"Why so secret?" he asked.

"I no want somebody tell Papasan they see me with G.I.," she said. "Papasan get very angry."

They ate breakfast of hot rice, soup, salmon, at a nearby restaurant. She had tea and he was very happy when the girl offered him cohe (coffee). A cab took them to the dock, just a few minutes away.

"We can take the steam boat or we can get small row boat and row to sacred island," she said. "If we take row boat we can cruise through the Torii. That very good thing."

"Then we'll take a rowboat," he said. They walked down the pier and she talked with a man on the dock for a few moments. "Three hundred yen for boat all day," she said.

"A real bargain," Frenchie agreed, paying the man.

They got into the boat, Emison in front and Frenchie in the middle with the oars. He floundered a moment, but soon the task of rowing came back to Frenchie and they were on their way. It was a small light boat and the lake was as smooth as glass. The sun was up now and Frenchie loosened his tie.

It wasn't long, about twenty minutes, and as they neared the island, a large sailing ship passed them, the family aboard the ship waved at them as they passed and Emison and Frenchie waved back. Now Frenchie could see the famous Torii, a free standing timber arch rising from the water. It was bright red and the sun shining on it made it seem almost on fire. Frenchie headed straight for the Torii and Emison became as excited as a schoolgirl on her first date. As they glided under the Torii she bowed and clapped her hands.

"Now we have beautiful day together," she said.

They docked the boat and suddenly the air was filled with the delicate fragrance of cherry blossoms. They were everywhere. Big and pink and beautiful, thousands upon thousands of them.

The entire island of Miyajima is sacred to the Japanese of the Shinto faith. The main shrine, called Itsukushima-jinja, is dedicated to the three daughters of Susano-o-no-Miloto, the Princesses Ichikishima, Tagori and Tagitsu. Records of the shrine date back to 811 A.D. Built on piles, the shrine seems to float on the sea when the tide rises. The buildings include the Main Shrine and several smaller connecting buildings and have been restored several times.

The Hall of a Thousand Mats was to the left of the shrine and it was said to have been built from the wood of a single camphor tree. The five-storied Pagoda close by was erected in 1407. On reaching the inside of the main shrine Emison clapped her hands and bowed very low. Many Japanese were performing this ritual. Many of them hung paper prayers on the iron lanterns.

After going through the main buildings they toured the beautiful spacious grounds. By law, no vehicles were allowed on the Island lest they frighten the sacred deer. Acres of beautiful virgin forest covered the Island.

They fed the holy horses and watched the sacred deer in the forest and then made the long climb up the hundreds of stone steps to the top of the Misen where a huge shrine was erected.

Here an eternal flame burned. They spent some time viewing the beautiful inland Sea below and Hiroshima in the distance.

They ate Sushi and rice and many other things Frenchie found it hard to identify, octopus and strange vegetables and many other strange things. They drank tea and, when they found themselves alone, Frenchie held her hand. The day was almost over as they returned to the boat and rowed back to Hiroshima where they took a cab back to the Hotel.

At the door, Frenchie took Emison by the hand.

"I have to get back to Eta Jima tonight," he said. "Will I ever see you again?"

"Tomorrow I go back Sapparo," she replied. "I don't sink so."

"Emison, what do you think of G.I.s now?" he asked.

"I sink maybe Papasan wrong. I sink maybe G.I.s very nice," she said softly.

"I'm glad," he said.

They parted outside the hotel and she went in alone. A few moments later he went to his room and after changing into his robe he headed straight for the bath. He would have one more go at that tub before returning to camp.

The water was hot and steaming. He felt relaxed and wonderful. His shoulders were a little stiff from all the rowing, but the hot water quickly eased his muscles. Suddenly the door opened and there she was. Her robe dropped to her feet and this time her firm breasts looked larger and even lovelier than he had remembered.

She stood there a full moment letting him take in her loveliness. She smiled at him and said nothing as she soaped and rinsed. In a moment she was finished and she glided into the pool beside him. He tried to hesitate but could do so no longer. He lunged for her and held her in his arms. He kissed her neck and explored her with his hands. She struggled and tried to get out of the tub but he held her close. He didn't hear the door open.

"AH SO!" Papasan screamed as he charged toward the tub.

Frenchie released Emison, jumped from the tub, grabbed his robe and ran to his room where he quickly dressed and headed for the boat to Eta Jima.

Papasan scolded his daughter as they continued their bath together.

"You right, Papasan, G.I. no good. You very smart man."

In quick Japanese Papasan grunted, "G.I. no good, Number 8 evil."

They sat silently in the steaming tub and finally Emison broke the silence. "Papasan," she asked. "Why G.I. seem so good and then act so bad?"

Papasan dunked his long goatee in the steaming water and thought for a long time. "Emison," he finally said. "Maybe some G.I. good all time. Maybe some G.I. bad all time. Maybe some G.I. good sometime and bad sometime, but Emison, I want you remember this, all time G.I. no good for you. You understand, Emison, you stay away from G.I."

"Hai, yes, I understand Papasan," she nodded. "You very smart man. Emison stay away from G.I."

14

Inspection

The sun was shining and there was a fresh cool breeze coming in off the sea as the men stood at attention as Captain Thompson relished the feeling of power he felt each morning at Reveille.

"There will be no passes tonight." He paused to watch the sad news sink in. "You men will get ready for a barracks inspection at 1000 tomorrow. There will be a general quarters inspection, including foot lockers. Any man getting a gig on inspection will lose his pass for two days."

Corporal Tuttle seemed pleased with the thought of an inspection. He held his enthusiasm until classes were over and the men had marched back to their quarters.

"We're going to have a real inspection, men," he announced. "Foot lockers and all. Each and every one of you is going to pass that inspection. We'll all get the same kind of razors and shoe polish and shaving cream and after-shave lotion and the same color washcloths and then we'll lay it out exactly the same. We'll have the sharpest looking foot lockers in the whole camp."

"That's swell Tuttle," Louie sneered. "I suppose you're going to buy all that crap."

"Why, no. You men will buy your own."

"That'll be a cold day in hell when I buy a bunch of crap just to pass an inspection," Louie said, his eyes glowing with fierce indignation.

"We all bought our own at Leadership School," Tuttle said.

"Well this ain't Basic Training or Leadership School, Tuttle, this is the Army and the book doesn't say we have to spend a lot of money just to pass an inspection. I'll clean the floor and make my bed and that's it. What's the deal anyway, how can we stand inspection and be at class tomorrow at the same time?"

"That is the nice part about it. We don't have to attend the inspection. We just leave our footlockers open. The Captain will make the inspection while we're at class." Tuttle smiled. He knew the men would be happy with this.

"Like hell," Louie said. "I've got a lock on my footlocker and when I'm not here the footlocker stays locked. What's the Captain going to do, kick us out of class? Nothing I'd like better."

"But the orders are--"

"Listen little fellow," Charlie said. "That Captain is always giving some kind of screwy order. If he wants to hold an ispection, than he can hold it according to the book. This isn't basic training. We're not a bunch of recruits. There are things the Captain can order and there are things he can't. One of the things he can't order is for me to leave my private property unlocked, unless someone is here to guard it for me. Now you can do what you want to tomorrow. You can lay your watch on your bed with a 'Take Me' sign. As for me and the rest of the fellows, we will clean up and make our beds. If the Captain wants to see inside those footlockers he can hold an inspection while we're here. Besides, there's nothing we'd enjoy more than fuckin' up so badly that we all have to blow this joint."

Tuttle shook his head and marched to the latrine. He located several buckets, half a dozen G.I. brushes and two mops. It wasn't easy but he finally made it. He walked into the barracks room with two buckets full of water, the mops and some brushes.

"What are the brushes for?" Louie asked.

"To scrub the floor," Tuttle replied.

"Now just a damn minute. Nobody said we were going to eat off that floor. It's just to walk around on. A damp mop will do the job just fine."

"But I thought we could use G.I. soap and then get a little bleach and with some sand paper and wax we can really make these floors pass inspection."

"Now wait a minute Tuttle," Louie said. "If the army wanted these floors finished and waxed then they would give us varnish and wax. I don't see where they gave us anything."

"But at Leadership School--"

"Now don't tell me about that La De Da School again," Louie said disgustedly. "Just take it easy and use a damp mop like the rest of us. If you get the crud up off the floor, that is all you have to do. Clean up the butts, get the gum from under the bed, dust off your locker and that's it. If you can't pass an inspection by doing that, then you're just not going to pass the inspection anyway. Those officers have already decided if you're going to pass an inspection or not. If they want to find dust, they find dust. If they want to find a dirty footlocker, they find it." Louie turned, grabbed a wet mop, quickly mopped his area, took a rag, wiped off this footlocker and clothes locker, checked under his cot for gum. In two minutes he was finished. He smiled, brushed off his hands and lay down on his sack, ready for whatever might come.

Tuttle rubbed, scrubbed, shined and shined some more. He carefully laid out his footlocker with items he had purchased at the P.X. just for the occasion. Next morning, he was still putting the finishing touches on things when the men fell out to march to class. Every footlocker was locked with the exception of one. It shined and glistened. It smelled of cologne so strongly that it stunk up the whole room.

When the men returned from class at noon they found a list on the bulletin board.

"The following men failed inspection this morning," it read. "Their passes will be pulled for two days. The reason for this action is that footlockers were not displayed as ordered." The list included the names of every man but one. Corporal Tuttle.

Tuttle read the list and smiled. "Ya see," he said.

"Yup," the men replied in unison.

"He's done it again, just like we figured he would. Put his big fat foot right in his mouth again," Frenchie laughed.

"Looks like it's time for another penny Black Jack game fellows," Frank suggested.

"Right after chow," Louie announced. "Class A uniforms, and don't forget the cards Charlie."

"Where are you fellows going?" Tuttle asked.

"Don't you worry about it," Louie replied.

"But your passes."

"Passes, asses. Just stick around little fellow and you will learn a little about army regulations."

"But the Captain..."

"Screw the Captain," Louie said. "He's just a misplaced civilian. Corporal, tonight he will learn a little about the Army's Regulations on Inspections."

Colonel Fizbee happened to be looking out the window as the men marched up his front walk. He was extremely pleased to see his Black Jack playing buddies.

"Come on in fellows. Why, it's been almost a week. I put a couple cases of beer on ice yesterday, just hoping you'd all come back."

"We've got a little more business for you Colonel." The men filed into the Colonel's home. "The Captain has pulled all of our passes this time. He pulled an illegal inspection and we thought you might be willing to help us teach him the inspection regulations." Charlie motioned the men to sit around the card table. "We'll tell you all about it while we play cards."

"Swell, men. Just tell old Fizbee your troubles and if you're right, then I'm with you."

After 45 minutes play Colonel Fizbee was ahead 16 cents and he was feeling quite jolly.

"Your passes are as good as in your hands," the Colonel said. "I'll call the Captain and have him meet you at his office with your passes in a few minutes."

"That is great, Colonel," the men replied.

Colonel Fizbee went into the other room and picked up the telephone. "Captain Thompson, this is Colonel Fizbee. Seems like you've done it again, Captain. About those men's passes Captain, I think you'd better run over to the office and give the passes back. I know about the inspection, Captain. Uh Huh, it was the foot lockers wasn't it? Locked? Of course they were locked. You don't leave your foot door open when you leave do you? Now listen, Captain, if you care to hold a footlocker inspection that is fine, but you'd better make sure the men are present. What if something is stolen? Did you realize that you would be responsible for every article missing? You didn't? These regulations are for your protection as well as the men's and I suggest that you spend a little time studying those regulations, Captain. Now about these passes, I realize that you are having your dinner right now so take your time getting over to the office. Just make sure you're there in the next ten minutes. Now just a minute, Captain, remember that you are now holding those men's passes illegally. I'm not sure that I can convince them not to make a case out of this, unless you get over there right away. Fine Captain. That is fine."

Fizbee came back into the room where the men sat silently listening to his every word.

"It's done," he said. "Just get over to the Captain's office and you'll all get your passes back. And don't forget, you're always welcome here. I haven't had so much fun playing Black Jack since I was a Second Lieutenant over in France in the First World War. Hurry back men, you're always welcome here."

The men marched directly to the Captain's office. The Captain was waiting, passes in hand. He didn't say a word. He seemed to be in deep thought. Sticking out of his back pocket was a copy of Army Manuel 100V. Army Regulations. The Captain had decided to do a little studying himself.

15

Concerto

Boots they nicknamed him. A good name considering the fact that he worked on his boots every day and he had the best shined boots on the post. The fact is, he was the best dressed soldier on Eta Jima and every item of his uniform was customized and spotlessly maintained. His real name was Henry Washington Smith and he was the only black man in the class. His home was in Detroit. His inclusion in the class was as a part of the Army's new plan for integration. Until this time the army had segregated blacks and maintained separate all black regiments. Korea and the Korean Conflict was a new venture into integration in the armed forces of the United States Army.

Boots knew a lot about integration. He'd been beat up in a race riot in Detroit, 1941 when he was just a kid.

He would never forget the crazy look some fellows had when they kicked him and called him Nigger. Then the National Guard came in to Detroit and things quickly cooled off. Things were getting better in Detroit by the time he was drafted. He was feeling pretty good about life. Though there were still a lot of prejudices. Getting jobs and things weren't exactly easy but he felt pretty good about his future when Uncle Sam sent him his greetings.

Then he went to Texas and he learned about riding in the Jim Crow section of the bus and after a while he got so he just stayed at camp and tried to be a good soldier. Then in Korea, after a few weeks he got on a really equal basis with the fellows in his outfit. They liked and trusted him and with all his courage, he was a good man to have around.

Then their squad got hit real bad on a patrol and grenades were flying everywhere.

"Then Boots went nuts," the fellows say. "It's like he figures the enemy can't shoot him or something. Bulling his way forward he fired his B.A.R. like crazy. Pretty soon there's dead Chinks all over the place and then powerful Boots grabs his white Sergeant, who's got a slug in his leg, and carries him all the way back to the command post. Gets him all the way back and they're giving blood to the Sergeant and everything when somebody sees that Boots is bleeding too. Got two slugs in his arm. And think of it, he carried this Sergeant a couple of thousand feet, up a hill and all." That's what the fellows said about Boots in the Infantry.

Boots wanted to be back in the Infantry, or else, back in Detroit. Things were swinging when Uncle sent the word. He had another nickname in Detroit. BeBop, the coolest drummer to come out of Cass Tech. He was "Giggin" all the time, one nighting, getting pick-jobs real steady. Dances, weddings, even labor rallies and political parties. Since he started singing Bop the jobs poured in. Sure he was a good drummer but his Be-Bop singing made him twice the attraction. Then Uncle gave him the word and into the Army he came.

He'd hoped for Special Service or an Army Band but he found he was in competition with drummers from name bands. When he finally resigned himself to being a rifleman, he decided to be the best there was. All through Basic Training he strived to have his uniform a little neater, his shoes a little shinier and his rifle a little cleaner than the others. Then in Korea he went at killing a little harder than the others. Not that he really hated the enemy. That was something he never really understood, but he worked the whole thing out in his head as a religious matter. To him Communism was atheism and therefore, in a way, he was fighting for the preservation of Christianity. That way it was like the Crusades or something. Fighting for Christ. And when you got right up there where the killing was going on, you had to have something to hang on to and for him this was a pretty good thing to hang on to. After all, politics and Harry Truman never came on very strong for Boots and so working this out as simply a religious war made it a little more worthwhile.

All that crap the army was passing out about stopping the flow of communism didn't impress Boots much when he knew darn well that no one was doing much about the Communists who were holding meetings right in the open in Detroit. It seemed kind of silly to be getting killed over a bunch of smelly rice paddies. Doing it all for Christianity at least gave it a purpose.

Being out of combat now and attending school made Boots come back down to earth a little and after a few weeks of classes he suddenly missed his drums very much. He checked the local bands over but they depressed him. Somehow they couldn't get the feeling for American music. Tempo meant nothing to these Japanesee musicians and they just struggled along trying to get the melody and the rhythm be damned.

Boots was sitting in Number One Beer Hall drumming on the table and trying to follow the complete lack of beat that the band was demonstrating. It bugged him too much and so when he finished his beer he left the hall and headed down the road that ran along the shore. He felt like wailing. His head was bursting with wild, creative drum solos. He could solo for a half hour right now without a break.

Blues. The "You Name It" Blues. The "Wish I was Home in Detroit" Blues. "The stars are bright, the moon is new, I'd like to do 10 choruses of 'How High' for you, but no one picks up on what I'm puttin' down," kinda blues.

He was on the road now. Walkin' slow and lookin' at the sea and the stars and the moon and being overcome by the sudden silence. After the noise of the cabaret the night was like instant quiet. Like covering your head with a pillow. Now he felt lonely but kind of peaceful too. He started a beat by snapping his fingers for a moment and then he tried his long unused scat voice on the quiet night air.

"By--oop be a da de op oh dele--O" right on down the road through eight choruses of "How High the Moon." He had picked up the beat and with it his step and now he was a couple of miles down the road and coming into a small village. People looked at him and smiled and he kept right on singing and smiling as he walked. Now a couple of children fell in behind him and followed and when he reached the far end of the village there were at least a dozen. They called to him as he started to go further and he stopped and was amazed at the happy looks on the children's faces. "Sing" one of the older children said and Boots squatted down and the kids all gathered around him. Once again he started snapping his fingers, this time in a quick beat and the children began clapping their hands in rhythm. "Oh sweet and lovely lady be good." "Shooby Dooby Be Op Ba Du Ba Le La De Da." The kids all smiled and kept on claping out the beat. The crowd grew and someone sensing Boot's need handed him a metal can and a stool. Suddenly the can became the drum that Boots wanted. He sat down on the stool and worked with his newly fashioned drum for a moment, feeling out the tones as one would on a bongo drum. Once he had it tested, he did a chorus of "Big Noise from Waneka." Then he went on to wilder things. Now the older people came closer and soon the entire population of the tiny village was gathered around Boots, keeping the beat while Boots wailed long into the night. "It's was the wildest," Boots would have said, but for some reason he kept the Concert to himself, when he finally returned to the Base. "A three hour session--all solo." Everyone in town seemed to dig what Boots was putting down. After the third number they started applauding and from then on they cheered at every number he did. "Like Carnagie Hall," Boots thought. "Only at Carnagie Hall you only draw a few of the people who live in New York and you pack the hall."

As a closing number, Boots had started out tapping a very deliberate slow blues beat and you could just sense that he was setting up just the right mood for the audience.

The entire group of villagers picked up the beat and within a few seconds he had them all moving slowly from side to side rocking in place to the steady powerful rhythm.

When he had it set just right, he began.

"Oh beautiful," he sang quietly.

"For spacious skies, for amber waves of grain."

He raised his head up just a bit and continued.

"For purple mountained majesties,

Upon the fruited plains."

And now Boots stood up proud and tall and looked up to the skies and sang out, loud, with his best blues voice,

"America! America! God shed his grace on thee!"

There were tears now, forming in his eyes, and all of that homesickness that he had been holding inside him, and all of that burning love that he felt for his country came pouring out in the words that he sang now--

"And crowned thy good

With brotherhood

From Sea to shining Sea."

There was no applause now. Just the purest silence which is sometimes a greater tribute than all the cheering in the world.

Boots bowed to the crowd and they all bowed back as he turned and began his walk back down the dirt lake road.

The small children followed him to the far end of the village and then they stopped and waved to him as he continued on down the road.

"Sayanara Misser Be-Bop," they called, and Boots waved back and grinned and called back, "I'll dig you later, children."

16

Man Among Men

Frank Tucker, "Lover Boy Tucker", he liked to be called. A real man with the ladies. That was a laugh. He wasn't too much of a man at all. It was a bluff he ran and somehow he needed the fellows to think that the women were wild about him. Frank Tucker, star quarterback of his high school football team. For a month he was the star and then he had the prettiest girl in town gushing over him. He played Gung-Ho football and in the 4th game of the season he broke his knee, and then the prettiest girl in town stopped gushing. Frank never got over it, not really.

After that something changed in Frank. He took up girls as a hobby and his main objective was to get every girl in town in bed and then tell her what a pig she was. Pretty nutty, he'd take the sweetest thing he could find and fill her up with words of love and marriage and anything else he had to to get his way, and then when he scored he'd go looking for something else.

Somewhere he'd read that there were only two kinds of girls, "Those who do and those who don't. Those who do, you take out with a bottle, have your way and forget about and those who don't you marry." Well, he wasn't about to be married and he wasn't about to believe those who said they don't.

His episode with the lost combat boots make Frank a little more careful with his shoes but he made the rounds every weekend picking out the prettiest girls he could find and then treating them just as badly as he could. He was amazed at the abuse the girls were willing to take from him. Especially Teriko. Whenever he came into town, Teriko was there, standing and waiting for him. But whenever he had the price of another girl he would leave Teriko standing there. He seemed to want to hurt her and every other living female. Teriko was patient and understanding. Even when Frank went on his wild experiment.

The idea didn't come to Frank Tucker right away. It took a couple of weeks to really take shape in his mind. There he was, a "Tiger" in the midst of 300 desirable available young things. At the going rate of 300 yen per engagement, he could sample the entire population for an investment of about 90,000 Yen. Roughly $250. A modest sum, indeed, considering what he would be achieving. Think of the distinction that would go with such an accomplishment. He would be a man among men. An idol among Idolaters.

The fact that he would be on Eta Jima for only 10 weeks and that two weeks had already passed didn't occur to him. The absolute physical and mathematical impossibility of the whole scheme was lost from sight. He was a man with a mission.

Although two weeks had already passed, they had not been a total loss to the project. He had already tallied up a score of 18, thanks to nightly passes and an outstanding scoring achievement on a weekend pass.

Frank Tucker was fast becoming known in town as a "Skippy" Honsho" and a "Butterfly Boyson." The first few weeks he tried to remember the girl's names but he soon realized the futility of it. After that he started using a number system.

"Twenty one, twenty two, twenty three. Wow, what a night."

"Twenty four, twenty five, twenty six." He was losing weight. Teriko was at the gate waiting patiently, but each night he passed her by. She said nothing but you could see that her heart was breaking.

"Twenty seven, twenty eight. Twenty nine can wait." Frank began to feel like a man shooting rabbits at a rifle range. Every time he knocked one down, another jumped up in its place and Frank was running out of ammunition.

"Twenty nine was fine, but enough for one night."

"Thirty was flirty. Think I'll take a day off and rest up."

Every night after chow Frank would get his pass to go to town and then spend considerable time wandering up and down Cherry Street choosing his bedmate. Every night he would see Teriko and she began to mean something special to him. It was a funny feeling for Frank, he thought of a girl as an instrument of gratification and yet somehow Teriko was becoming something different. The more he passed her by, the more loving she looked the next time he saw her.

He recalled how she had returned his money that first night they made love and he realized that she was the only one to do that. Somehow he wished that he could have that same experience again, but it wasn't his policy to go back for seconds. Once he had put a girl in her place he went on to greener fields. Frank kept running up his tally. By the time he reached forty he felt fifty years old. He realized now that it was time to sit down and make an honest evaluation of the project and its chance for success.

For two nights he wandered up and down Cherry Street with paper and pencil in hand, making a head count. (A tail count would have been a more appropriate name for it.) Not counting those engaged at the time of the census he counted a total of 241 girls. It was then only a simple process of arithmetic. He hadn't even made a dent in the sum total and there he was, half dead from exhaustion. The project was impossible from the beginning, he reasoned. Why, it would take a damn good man 6 to 8 months to make his way around the Island and there he was trying to do it in just 10 weeks. He went back to camp and mulled the whole thing over in his mind. The next evening when he came through the gate Teriko was waiting as usual. She smiled at him and her eyes showed her love and sorrow. This time instead of passing her by, he stopped.

"What are you waiting for Teriko?" he asked.

"For you Frank." she said, holding her head up unashamed.

"But why?" he asked.

"Because when I give you presento, I give you my heart." Tears came now. All of the sorrow of being passed up night after night welled up in her and come to the surface in tears.

Frank was embarrassed. He noticed the other G.I.'s passing by and he wanted to be alone with Teriko.

"Where can we go?" he asked. "I want to talk to you."

Her sobbing stopped and she looked up hopefully. "We can go my girlfriend's house if you want. She go Hiroshima for week and I can get her room."

The two walked hand in hand down Cherry Street and then around a narrow lane to her small house. Teriko talked with an old woman and then slid open a bamboo door and Frank took off his shoes and carried them in with him.

They said nothing for a full moment and then Teriko sat next to Frank, took his hand in hers and asked, "Why you Butterfly, Frank? What are you looking for?"

The question floored Frank. Why was he a Butterfly? What was he looking for? "For kicks." he answered, knowing it was untrue.

"What kicks?" she asked, looking very confused.

"Thrills. Something new. Just Kicks." Frank said.

"Teriko no give you kicks, Frank?" she asked, looking very disappointed.

"Sure, you're good for kicks, Teriko. But after you've had those kicks, you've had them."

Teriko was all the more confused. "Teriko no understand. You don't like Teriko." Her eyes now pleaded for a kind reply.

"Sure I like you Teriko, but I like to experiment too."

"The girls say you call them pig after short time. Why you call girls pig, Frank?"

"Listen Teriko, what is this, the fifth degree or something?"

"No fifth degree, Frank. Teriko try to understand, that's all."

"Well, they are pigs. Any girls that go to bed with me are pigs. A bunch of dirty pigs, that's what."

"I no understand Frank. You want girl to go to bed with you. Why you say pig if you want girl to go to bed and she do?"

"You don't get it, Teriko. Girls aren't supposed to go to bed with a guy until they get married. If they do then they're pigs."

"Then why you try to get all girls in bed and never want to marry? Teriko no understand. You think Teriko pig?"

Teriko had stopped her sobbing but now she started again. Big tears came running down her cheeks and the sight disturbed Frank. She looked at him and her heart was burning with love. "I no want you think I pig, Frank. I want you love Teriko. You think Teriko Pig?"

"Let's forget this pig thing, Teriko. I think you're just fine. Now whatta ya say we get some tea or something."

"Maybe we go outside, you catch some other girl. You biggest Butterfly on Island."

"Not tonight. I need a rest Teriko. I need a long rest and I need time to think."

"Teriko make tea right here and you stay with Teriko. I let you rest Frank. I let you rest real good."

She went out and came back with some coals to start the Hibachi and soon she had water boiling for tea. It was good and Frank laid back and relaxed for the first time in weeks. He spent the night with Teriko and she did not press him for affection. She rubbed his back and made him more tea. He returned to camp in the morning feeling rested and his mind was more at peace than it had been for some time.

For the next four nights Frank had overnight passes and each night he would eat and sleep with Teriko and not once did he touch her. It was a rare experience. He talked with her, learned Japanese songs and they drank tea while she rubbed his back. He told her about his high school days, about his folks and finally about the girl who threw him over when he was no longer a football star. It was the first time he had ever told anyone about the girl that had put him down. Somehow, after he told her he didn't want to make all of the girls on the island any longer. It didn't seem necessary.

When Teriko's girlfriend returned from Hiroshima, Frank gave Teriko enough money to rent a room and buy a little food. Teriko no longer walked the streets. She waited each day for the moment Frank would arrive and then her life would take on new meaning. She was alive and she was proud and happy. Frank assured her every night that she was a very nice girl and by no means a pig. They lived together like man and wife and Frank never looked at another girl. They both knew that Frank would be on his way at the end of the ten weeks but it didn't matter. Life was so sweet for them and they took from it every bit of happiness that they could find.

One night, in the ninth week, Frank was feeling especially content and Teriko was gently massaging his neck. "Teriko," he asked, "Remember that night we met. Remember how you gave me back my Yen?"

Teriko blushed a little remembering her past. "I remember Frank. I say 'presento' and give you back money."

"Tell me Teriko. Was I really that good?"

"You very good, Frank. But that not why I give you back Yen. You look unhappy then Frank. Very unhappy. I think maybe yen bring you happiness,"

"Not Yen, Teriko. You bring me happiness." Frank took her in his arms and kissed her. "Just you bring me happiness Teriko, just you."

17

Phone Call Home

Ben Reardon had been overseas six months. His wife had presented him with an eight-pound boy three months after he shipped out. He received the first picture of little Roger while recouperating from wounds in the hospital at Kobe. Mail had a way of remaining far behind when you were on the move and Ben hadn't stopped moving since he was drafted. First it was Camp Custer at Battle Creek, Michigan, then to Fort Riley, Kansas for six weeks, after that it was Fort Bliss at El Paso, Texas. Eight weeks later he got home for a 10-day leave and from there he made short stops at Seattle, Washington; Camp Drake in Toyko, Japan; Inchon, Korea, and then northward to the Chorwon Valley where he tried dodging Chinese fire power for four months.

He complained about all of that moving but he should have kept moving a little longer, he would not have been occupying the spot where enemy mortar shell shrapnel was flying. When he caught a sizeable chunk in his left shoulder he hoped that it would be the ticket that would let him travel back to the States and his new family. He kept hoping that all the time the Army kept moving him from one hospital to another. First, the M.A.S.H. unit at Won-dong-po, then southward to Taegu where they removed the Shrapnel before strapping him to a litter and flying him to Kobe, Japan. After a month recouperating and physical therapy at Nara, Japan, he traveled to Eta Jima.

Getting moved, hit, moved, carved up, moved, resting up, moved, even though he was writing home every day possible, none of his mail caught up with him for nearly six weeks. It makes it really rough on a guy to go through all of that hell without having a buddy let alone a letter from home.

He missed the letters from his loving little Ruth most of all. He wasn't sure how his wife was going to take his injury. He kept haunting the Army Postal service every day with a heavy heart, hoping against hope that he would get some mail. He knew that if he ever got his mail he was going to tell the whole damned Army to forget him while he took time off to catch up on the news from home.

Ben hadn't even been to town yet after arriving at Eta Jima. He'd been to the Post Movie a dozen times and walked around the base 'til he knew it by heart, but always found his way back to the base Post Office whenever there was a chance that more mail might have arrived. One nice thing about being on Eta Jima at this time of year was the fact that the Cherry Blossoms were in full bloom. He could look up at the nearby mountainsides and watch the natives searching the shady side of the mountain for mushrooms and they would carry baskets full back down. Sheep were grazing nearby in open spaces at lower levels. Ben could look in the other direction to the sea and watch divers disappear beneath the surface and remain out of sight for what seemed like an impossible period of time, then reappear with a fish or some other edible from somewhere beneath the waves.

Ben spent a lot of time at the Post Beer Hall as there was really nothing in town for him. Beer was cheaper on the base and a guy had to think about his wife and new son at home. He did not want to go into town for fear he would be tempted to partake of some of the goodies the other guys were always talking about.

It was a Saturday afternoon and most of the fellows were in town. Things were too quiet around the barracks. The men had been paid that morning and some had got into a poker game while waiting for passes. Ben had done all right in the game, picking up an extra forty dollars with three good hands in a row. It almost made a very lonely guy want to go into town with the gang and celebrate. After all, he had been sending Ruth almost every cent he got paid and it wasn't like he was holding out on her or anything. He guessed it wouldn't hurt to go into town and look around and see what it was like. After all of his traveling he had begun to think of himself as a professional tourist, he might just as well go see what this town was like. It wouldn't hurt, besides he was lonely and he could be with some buddies if he went. He decided it might just get him out of the bored mood that was bugging him. He laid on his bunk and kicked the idea around for a while, then went by the mail chute once more to make sure that nothing had arrived in the hour since he had checked last.

"I could go to town and have a beer and just look the place over a little," he mused. He took out his wallet for the thousandth time to admire the picture of his wife and new son. His eyes kept going to those forty newly acquired one dollar bills bulging his wallet and that decided it. He'd go to town for just a couple of hours.

Ben had barely walked through the front gate of the base and entered when a cute little Japanese girl approached, "Do Co E Ke No, G.I.?"

Just what he was afraid of, Cherry Street was in full swing. She would have been jail bait back home. A little too much lipstick maybe, but she sure was pretty. Funny how it works, but the longer it's been since you've seen a woman the prettier they get.

Ben just stood and stared for a full minute, then he realized that she was waiting for a reply. "Huh?" he asked.

"Do Co E Ke No. Where you go G.I.?" she tried again.

Ben looked up and down the street, none of his buddies had stuck around to save him. "I'm just going into town for a beer, that's all, just a beer."

She took his arm and snuggled her warm body close to his and turned her big brown eyes up to look deep into his mind. "Me hot to go," she said softly.

"Huh?" Ben stammered.

"Me hot to go," she repeated. "You com'on my house, OK G.I.?"

Shaking his head, his desires thirsting in every cell of his body, "Unh, Uh," Ben repeated. "I'm just out for a beer."

"You Cherry boy?"

"No." His shaking body emitted a nervous laugh. "I'm married." He forced his body to try to walk away, the throb in the center of his body was going out to his extremities in waves of heat.

About a hundred feet down the street a second beauty approached him. Ben saw her coming and some of his courage was coming back, "Don't waste your time baby, I'm married and just out for a beer." She turned and went back to her post by the cabaret. A half block down the street the Tennessee Waltz was blasting over the speakers. It caught Ben's attention. It was the song that Ruth and he thought of as their song. He suddenly felt terribly homesick. Ruthie had sung that song to him on the last night of his leave. "God, how I need her!" he thought as almost blindly, he entered and found a booth towards the back where he could wallow in his loneliness.

"Biru?" a girl asked.

"Ya a beer, a real cold beer," Ben replied, his eyes glued to the curves of her body as she walked away. A cold shower would have been more appropriate at the moment. The girl silently disappeared to the back room to return in a moment with a quart bottle of Asahi Beer, a glass and a small dish of unsalted peanuts. She carefully poured the beer into his glass and sat the peanuts beside the glass.

"One hundred eighty yen," she said.

Ben fished in his pocket and came out with a rumpled G.I. bill and tried to hand it to her. She pushed it away, "No good, need yen."

"I forget to get yen, won't a dollar do?"

"OK G.I., Rickshaw driver make change for you."

She quickly ran to the door to return in a minute with a handful of change and counted out 180 yen and gave Ben the rest. She stood looking at him for a long moment until he set his glass down. She sat down across the little booth table from him, tipped the bottle up and refilled his glass. He took a cigarette and her soft gentle hand was right there with a lighter. He took another little sip of beer and she again filled the glass. He began to get a little nervous and tried to divert her eyes from the slight rise of her breasts at the top of her blouse. "Look, don't you have other tables to wait on?"

"Just you," she smiled and pointed to a group of four G.I.s at another booth where four waitresses eagerly waited to serve them. "Every G.I. get own waitress. Very special service."

"Well, you make me nervous just sitting there staring at me, do you want a beer?" Part of Ben was hoping she would say no, another part was yearning to enjoy her femininity.

"No like beer, like cider. Cider only 40 yen."

The girl smiled gratefully and ran quietly to the back room, returning with a bottle of cider and a glass. "Allegato."

"What's that?" Ben asked. "Alligator?"

"Not Alligator--Allegato. That mean sank you."

"Oh ya. Well, you're welcome."

"Say, do I tas I mas I," she suggested.

Ben laughed, not quite understanding. "Don't touch mustache."

She started to snicker but covered her mouth to hide the laughter. "Do I tas I Mast Ey."

"Ya, I guess so," Ben agreed not understanding just what she meant.

The song playing on the little portable record player came to an end and one of the girls from the other table got up and went over to the record player. "Irene," one of the G.I.s yelled. "Ya, Irene," another shouted.

The four G.I.s had apparently been there quite a while. Their shirts were partly unbuttoned and they all looked a little unsteady. When the girl found the record she put it on and the G.I.s huddled together like a barber shop quartet and boisteriously sang:

"Irene, Goodnight Irene, Irene Goodnight.

Goodnight Irene, My sex machine,

I'll see ya in my dreams.
I gave Irene a wristwatch
She swallowed it one day,
Now Irene is taking Ex-Lax
Just to pass the time away."

They all started laughing and after a quick sip of beer picked up the song again and continued,

"Irene, Goodnight Irene. Irene Goodnight
Goodnight Irene My Sex Machine,
I'll see you in my dreams."

By the time the record finished Ben's beer was gone. The girl noticed, picked the bottle up and tipped it up as though it were a cow's teat and acted like she was stripping it dry. It was a ritual they all performed. She looked into Ben's eyes quizzically, "Another Biru?"

"Ya, another beer and play the Tennessee Waltz again, will you?"

"Sure, G.I., you like Tennessee Wartz?"

"My wife likes it."

"Your wife Stateside, G.I.?"

"Ya, I sure wish I was too."

"You live in Tenneshee, G.I.?"

Ben chuckled at that one, "No, I'm from Michigan."

"How come they no have Michigan Wartz? I get sick of Tenneshee Wartz. That's all G.I. play. Three records all the time. Tenneshee Wartz, Irene Goodnight and Com'ona My House."

"What song do you like?" Ben asked.

"Shina No Yoru (China Night), that beautiful song about Japanese soldier who is in China and very lonesome for Japanese girl back home. He sit by river and feel very, very sad."

"I sure know how he felt, I feel the same way about my wife," Ben lamented.

"I play record for you, G.I." Ben watched the movement of her slender body as she walked over to the record player and felt pleased as she turned off Irene, right in the middle of the song. The other G.I.s were a little disturbed but not enough to interfere with thoughts of Irene as their sex machine.

Ben quickly finished his second beer and ordered the third. He learned the girl's name was Michiko. "Micky some G.I.s call me. Some call me Mickey Mouse."

Mickey heard the strains of Tennessee Waltz and started to hum the tune for him. She had the disturbing habit of staring deep into Ben's soft blue eyes. "You dance, G.I.?"

"Sure I dance, Mickey Mouse."

They got up and walked to the center of the room where a small section was cleared for dancing. Mickey nestled her warm little body in Ben's arms and sang softly in his ear: "I was danshing with my darring to the Tenneshee Wartz,

"When an old friend --o I hoppened to shee."

Ben couldn't help smiling at the pronounciation, but really it didn't matter. For a moment anyway, he tried to make believe he was back home dancing with Ruthie. When they finished dancing Ben sat down to finish off his third beer.

Before he did however he started proudly showing Mickey the pictures of his wife and new son. He told her how it hurt not to be receiving her letters. He even told her about sending her all the money possible but he was only in town as a result of winning the forty dollars in a poker game.

"Why no telephone your wife. Cost maybe twenty-five dollars. It make you very happy."

"I never thought of that. Didn't even know you could. How can I make a call?"

"Other G.I. tell me you go to special telephone office on base."

Ben quickly finished his beer, gave Mickey the remaining yen laying on the table and told her to have her fill of cider.

"Thanks for the information," he said and almost leaned over to kiss her, thought better of it, turned and walked out of the Cabaret onto Cherry Street.

A girl immediately started toward him, "What you do now, G.I.?"

Ben smiled the broadest smile since leaving home. "I'm going to blow twenty-five dollars on a phone call to my wife."

It took him three hours to get the call through and when Ruthie finally answered she sounded terribly worried.

"Sure, I'm OK," he tried to assure her. "I just had to call and find out how you and Roger are. Everything is great now."

She'd been writing every day but she didn't get his new address until the previous week. Sure she loved him. More than ever and Roger was getting bigger, sleeping and eating real good now. Doctor said it was her worry about Ben that caused the baby to have a little problem at first. They only had time to say "I love you" a half dozen times before the three minutes were up and the operator cut in. Ben walked out of the telephone station feeling the best he had felt in a long time. He'd even heard his son Roger, cry.

18

Just For Now

Charlie was hooked. Just two weeks with Happy and he was sure that he could never again live without her. He'd been thinking about it constantly and there was only one solution, marriage. Not just-for-now, but just forever. He'd thought about the folks back home and how they'd talk, but he really didn't care. Just so he could be with Happy. That was all that was really important to him.

It was Sunday and he planned to meet Happy at noon, but he had attended the service at the Post Chapel and now he was determined to see the Chaplain and talk about his problem.

Reverend Peters had been overseas a long, long time. He loved G.I.s and knew their language. Just this morning he had nearly busted up the service with a story. "Men," he had said. "We now have a new preventative for Venereal Disease. It's called Noassatall. It's even better than Sulfa Denial." After that he gave a stirring speech on purity and the men loved it. When the service was over Charlie waited until the other men had walked away.

"Say Chaplain, could I talk with you a few minutes?"

"Sure soldier. What's on your mind?"

"Marriage. I mean, how do you go about marrying a Japanese girl?"

"Well, it's a little complicated, but it is possible. First there are several papers you have to fill out. Then the Army makes a check on the girl to see if she is in good health. They check her character and find out if she has ever been a prostitute and---"

"What if she has?"

"Then you can't marry her or take her into the United States."

"How do they determine if she's ever been a prostitute?"

"By the Health Cards they issue, that's one way. If she has ever obtained a Health Card then she is registered."

"Oh no." Charlie shook his head and hit his hand with his fist.

"Is she registered?"

"She just registered for me. You see she lived with this other G.I.

and he went home. Then I came along and just to prove to me that she was OK, she went and got this Health Card."

"That's the regulation soldier, they're awfully strict about it."

"What can I do then Chaplain?"

"Well you can marry the girl and stay here in the service."

"Oh no, I'm getting out just as soon as I can."

"Then forget about her. It's just one of those impossible situations. Morally you can't live with her without marrying her and legally you can't marry her and take her home with you. I suggest you just forget about her."

"But I love her."

"You asked my advice, Soldier, and you got it."

Charlie wanted to argue it out but there was no point in arguing with the army.

"Thanks Chaplain. I know you didn't write the regulation."

Charlie was disgusted. What kind of a spot was this to be in. He kicked the ground impulsively, turned and walked to where Happy was.

"Just-for-now," he thought, "is a damn site better than not at all."

19

Ben-Chan

Ben was getting a letter nearly every day now from Ruth and the more she wrote the more he wished he could get home. He'd been drafted for 24 months and they had put in a policy that any G.I. who had been in combat and returned home in time could be separated from the service after 21 months active duty. The trick was in getting home to get out early. There was a point system and you had to have a certain number of points to rotate home. A G.I. got four points a month for combat duty in Korea, two points for behind the line duty in Korea and one point a month in Japan. At this rate he'd be in for a full 24 months and it would be a another year before he'd see his new son.

If he could get only a few more months combat duty as an infantryman he'd be home in no time. The prospect of graduating from Clerk's School and getting a one point a month job made Ben all the more determined to seek a way back into the Infantry.

He was feeling homesick again and it was Saturday night. The barracks was nearly empty and so he decided to take a walk into town and maybe a beer and tell his troubles to Mickey.

This time he remembered and stopped into the P.X. and exchanged five dollars for yen. He walked through the gate and right past the eager young girls that called to him, straight to the Bar Swan where he had first talked with Michiko. He took a booth. The bar was quite crowded and as Ben sat down a pretty young thing greeted him and asked, "Birru?"

"Where is Mickey?" he asked.

"Mickey take two days off and go to Hiroshima," she replied. "You want Birru?"

"Not now, I'll take a walk around first."

Ben walked onto Cherry Street and headed down the street. Several of the fellows had told him about the fine band at Number One Beer Hall and so he thought he'd give a listen. A few girls on the street made Ben some rather attractive offers but he pretended not to hear them.

As Ben walked slowly up the high stairway that led to Number One Beer Hall he heard a faint noise that sounded like a sob. He stopped and listened. He waited a minute and then he heard the sob again. It came from the darkness down behind the stairway. Ben walked back down the steps and walked around to where the noise came from. It was a girl. A young girl, 18 maybe, small, not every pretty and her face was wet with tears. She was sitting in the dark corner crying her heart out. Ben hesitated a second and then he walked forward and leaned over to where the girl sat. "What's the matter?" he asked.

The girl cried a little harder and sobbed, "Never mind G.I., just go away."

Ben started to leave and the girl sobbed a little harder.

"Is there something I can do?" Ben asked.

"Never mind G.I.," the girl sobbed. "Not your problem."

Ben leaned over and slowly rubbed the girl's neck. "Come on now," he said. "It can't be that bad. How about talking it over with me. I'll buy you a beer or a cider."

The girl's crying slowed down a little and she stood up and looked into Ben's eyes. She was quite surprised. "Why you buy me a beer?" she asked.

"Because you look like you need someone to talk to and I guess, well, maybe I need someone to talk to too," he admitted.

They went to a small quiet sake house and Ben ordered two beers. The girl carefully dried her eyes and straightened her lipstick, then took her two index fingers and borrowing a little lipstick from her mouth she carefully distributed it on her cheeks. She brushed back her hair and then without the slightest hesitation, taking both breasts in her hands she pushed them a little higher under her sweater. This ritual completed she looked at the beer and at Ben and said, "Toxon Allegato. Many thanks."

"Don't touch the mustache," Ben replied.

The girl smiled for an instant and then sobbed a tiny sob still left over from her long cry.

"Now tell me your name and why you are crying," Ben suggested as she poured out the beer.

"Yoshiko. My name Yoshiko. Your name?"

"Ben. Now why are you crying?"

"Long, long story Ben. You no can help."

"Well look Yoshiko, I've got all night to listen. Maybe before you get done we can sit down and cry together. Now tell me your troubles."

"OK Ben, but you no can help. Nobody can help Yoshiko. Troubles too big. It start two year ago when I work in Teahouse at Kokura. I work as waitress and live with Papasan and Mamasan. I very nice girl and have no boyfriend or anysing, just work at teahouse and go home. Then one day G.I. paratrooper come to teahouse and smile at me. Pretty soon he come every day and after long time he talk me into come live in room with him. We no marry, but he keep saying "some day." Then after one year he come and say he go Stateside. I never see him after that."

She stopped talking and took a sip of beer. Then she continued. "When I go live with him my Papasan very pisto. He say no talk to him, no see him ever again. When I go live with G.I. I lose job at teahouse. G.I. go away and I go to Papasan and he get mad and hit me and say 'Go away forever.' So I take train to Hiroshima and hope to get job."

She started to cry again and Ben squeezed her hand and urged her to continue. "I no find job, get hungry and girl I meet tell me about Eta Jima. I come to Eta Jima and lady buy me American clothes and help paint my face and tell me to go catch G.I. I no good short time girl. No like catch G.I. I work three months and catch only couple G.I.s and Mamasan get mad and say I no good. I owe Mamasan toxon money for clothes and food and now I find out I have baby. No can have baby. Tomorrow go to hospital. Sayanara baby. Now I want to die."

Ben picked up the girl's beer bottle and filled her glass. He took out his cigarettes and offered her one. "No sank you, I don't smoke. I never drink Birru before but tonight you say you buy Birru so I try. Now my lip feel funny."

Ben lit a cigarette and took a deep puff. "You've sure got troubles Yoshiko. I was always brought up to believe that having an abortion was something awful but over here I guess it's legal."

"Hai, it's legal, but I no like lose baby. I wish I just die, that more easy. I no good short-time girl. No find job, no want live."

Ben sipped his beer and thought about it. He couldn't give the girl much encouragement, he sure didn't feel like taking on the job of changing the entire moral and economic structure of Japan. He took Yoshiko's hand and patted it and comforted her and told her, "You just take it easy. Life gets kinda rough for everybody once in a while but you just wait, something good will happen to you. That's life, up and down the hills. Things are going to be better for you Yoshiko, life is going to be a whole lot better. You just wait and see." He finished his beer and patted her a few more times and gave her a friendly smile. "Now I've got to get back to camp."

"What about your troubles, G.I.?" she asked.

"Forget them," he said. "I just found out that I don't have any troubles."

The next night Ben decided to walk into town for a beer again. It gave him something to do and it helped to kill the boredom and frustration that came with attending classes each day. As Ben walked through the gate a girl was waiting. This wasn't unusual but this girl had a very serious look on her face. She walked up to Ben and asked, "You Ben-san?"

"Ya I'm Ben," he replied.

"Hayaku (Hurry!) Yoshiko almost die, she cry for you. Please hayaku," she said excitedly.

Ben quickly followed the girl through several narrow alleys, and after a few minutes arrived at a large house containing many small rooms. The girl automatically removed her shoes and motioned to Ben to do the same. They went through a series of rooms and finally to a cold drafty room in the rear of the building. The room was dirty and had a foul smell. Apparently it was used as a storage room but they had thrown a mattress on the floor and on it lie Yoshiko. She looked terrible white and appeared to be in a coma.

"Ben-Ben," she called faintly.

Ben knelt down on the floor next to Yoshiko. "It's me, Yoshiko, it's Ben."

Yoshiko's mouth formed a faint smile and she gave a deep sigh of relief. Ben took her hand, it felt rather cold to him. He turned to the girl that stood in the doorway. "Get me something to warm this room up." The girl quickly left and returned with a Hibachi filled with white hot charcoal. Ben looked the room over. It was dirty and a bag of half rotten vegetables laid in the corner.

Yoshiko looked at Ben and tears rolled slowly from her eyes. "Baby gone now. Doctor operate at hospital and baby gone."

Ben sat silently a few moments and then took a towel that was lying nearby and wiped Yoshiko's forehead. Some of the tenseness had left her face and she appeared to be dozing.

He turned to the girl in the doorway, "This is a hell of a place for a sick girl, don't you have a clean room for her?"

"Mamasan very angry," the girl explained. "Yoshiko no pay Mamasan, no catch G.I. Mamasan say this only room for Yoshiko."

"I'm going back to camp and get something to clean this room up. If Yoshiko wakes up tell her I'll be right back."

Ben rushed back to camp and picked up some G.I. soap, a brush, some D.D.T. and a G.I. blanket. He stopped at the Post Exchange and bought a few small items, then on the way back to the house he picked up a half pint of Ackadami, a cheap, potent Japanese drink.

He quickly found the house, removed his shoes again and went in. Two hours later Ben had worked up quite a sweat. The room was now spotless. Yoshiko was in a deep sleep, she was no longer cold, in fact, perspiration was running from her forehead. Ben took a cool cloth and gently mopped her brow. She slowly opened her eyes and spoke, "Bensan, you make Yoshiko very, very happy. Last night I sink no want live, but you talk to Yoshiko and now I sink everysing be Dai Jobu (all right)."

Ben recalled what he had said and although he hadn't really believed those words apparently they had done Yoshiko a lot of good. "Pretty soon everysing Dai Jobu." Ben agreed.

Yoshiko looked anything but all right. Her skin was deathly pale and Ben was afraid to leave her. About 2300, Mamasan came back and said some nasty things that Ben didn't understand. She waved her arms and with her fingers she made the international sign that meant "shame on you." After a lot more yelling she held out her hand and demanded four hundred yen. Ben wasn't sure what it was all about. Did Mamasan think something funny was going on in the small room? Surely she knew that Yoshiko was in no shape for anything, especially that. She stood her ground and once again made a sound by rubbing her fingers together and showing her contempt for Ben. He didn't understand it but he reached into his pocket and peeled off four one hundred yen bills and gave them to Mamasan. She seemed satisfied and said, "Juta mote (just a minute)." Ben waited and in a few seconds she returned with a pillow and a blanket. Ben went back into the room and sat down. Yoshiko was awake and when she saw the blanket she smiled. "You stay?" she asked.

"I guess it won't hurt," Ben replied. "You might need somebody and I don't think Mamasan cares if you live or die."

Yoshiko took Ben's hand and held it in her own. When she looked at Ben some of the missing color returned to her cheeks. Ben took a pillow and blanket and laid beside Yoshiko. He was exhausted. The moment his head hit the pillow he drifted off to sleep. Yoshiko laid there gazing adoringly at Ben for a long, long time and then finally she too slept. It was a very, very happy kind of sleep.

Ben awoke with a start. Someone was knocking on the door and suddenly he remembered that he had not signed out for an overnight pass. He was technically A.W.O.L. He wiped the sleep from his eyes and opened the door. It was the girl who had directed him to the house the night before. "I bring somesing to eat," she softly announced.

Ben opened the door wider and the girl brought the tray in and sat it on the floor near Yoshiko. "Thanks," Ben said. "I mean Alligator." The girl laughed at Ben's joke and left the room.

Yoshiko tried to sit up but her strength just wasn't there. Ben looked at the tray. It certainly wasn't ham and eggs but the hot bean-curd soup smelled rather good. There was a large serving of rice and a pot of tea and two cups. Ben carefully fed the hot soup to Yoshiko and after a slow start she seemed to take more interest and in a few moments the soup was gone. Ben then tried his skill at handling rice with chopsticks. He wasn't much good but Yoshiko found it amusing. The steaming green tea certainly wasn't exactly the black coffee that Ben was used to, to start his day, but it tasted good and drove the sleepiness from his body.

When they had finished eating Ben checked his watch. He still had time to get back to camp and make reveille formation. Maybe if he was lucky he could get through the gate without being checked. Maybe the fellows had covered for him at bed check. He washed up, straightened his uniform and after making sure that Yoshiko was feeling much better he said his goodbyes and headed back to camp.

The M.P.s were busy giving information to a couple of officers in a jeep when he went through the gate. He was in luck. He headed straight for the assembly area and arrived just in time to make the reveille formation. Captain Thompson came marching briskly to the head of the formation and completed his ritual in the prescribed manner. When he had finished he looked sternly at the Personnel Class and said, "Private Ben Reardon, I want to see you immediately after this formation." The Captain looked back at the formation and then to Sergeant Riley, "Sergeant dismiss the men."

As the men filed back to the barracks Tom approached Ben, "What's the old man want with you, Ben?"

"I wonder."

"Well, it's not about not making bed check last night," Tom said as he smiled broadly. "Thanks to our pillows you came through bed check last night with flying colors."

Ben looked a little relieved. "Thanks Tom."

As Ben walked into the office Sergeant Riley quietly motioned for Ben to go back into the hallway. Riley came to the doorway and talked quietly into Ben's ear. "The old man just checked the overnight passes to see if you were on the list. You weren't."

"No I wasn't."

"Then he checked the bed check and it looked OK."

"Good."

"Just thought you'd like to know."

"Thanks," Ben said as he walked back into the office, through the Captain's private door and as he stood at attention he reported. "P.F.C. Ben Reardon reporting as ordered, Sir."

Captain Thompson returned the salute and finished reading the official looking directive on his desk. This done, he looked up at Ben who was still standing rigidly at attention. "At ease Private." Thompson looked Ben up and down and after a long moment of silence continued. "Didn't I see you going through the gates this morning, Private?"

"Perhaps, Sir," Ben replied.

Captain Thompson looked surprised at Ben's honesty. "Sitting up with a sick friend, Private?"

"How did you know?" Ben asked.

"They're always sitting up with a sick friend," the Captain said. "You were A.W.O.L. you know. I checked the overnight passes and you weren't on the list."

"I know Sir. I didn't intend to stay overnight but things just happened."

"I like your honesty Private. You're dismissed."

Ben was shocked. "You mean you're going to let it go Sir?"

"That's right, Private."

"But Sir, you're suppose to be a horse's---."

"That's my job, Private. Now, get out of here before I change my mind."

"Yes Sir." Ben snapped to attention and saluted smartly. He turned and as he reached the door he turned back again.

"And thank you, Sir," he said.

"By the way, Private, there isn't anything you'd like to tell me about a garbage can at my door, is there?"

"I don't know what you mean, Sir," Ben replied.

"You know Reardon, I think you really were up with a sick friend last night."

"Thank you Sir," Ben replied as he came to attention, saluted and marched out of the Captain's office.

20

The Plan

Eta Jima's location at the southern tip of Japan made it the logical spot for the Australian Army to use as a debarkation point for homeward bound, battle weary troops who had completed their tour of duty in Korea. There were only a few small groups each week and therefore the U.S. Army had agreed to house and feed the men as they were passing through. A group of ten such Australian soldiers had arrived that morning. It was Monday and the men in the clerk's class were in their ninth week of school. Two more weeks and they would graduate and then it was back to their outfits where they could look forward to serving in the Personell Offices.

This thought had occurred to Louis and he decided that the only way to get rid of the thought would be to hang a good one on. He consulted his billfold and found it empty. After a thorough search, he finally admitted to himself that his total resources amounted to thirty cents. Certainly this would not finance a trip to town and so in desperation he headed for the Army Post Beer Hall where canned beer could be purchased for ten cents.

After drinking two beers he felt no better and so he parted with the last barrier he had between himself and absolute poverty. Sadly he sat alone in the corner of the beer hall at a large table. It was the only table left and all the other seats were occupied. Louie sat, slowly sipping on his last can of beer when the beer hall door opened and in walked the ten Aussie soldiers. They wore brown berets cocked to one side of their heads and they looked thirsty. After ordering, they spotted the table in the corner, occupied by only Louie.

"Say Matey, mind if we share your table?"

Louie looked up from his now empty can and replied, "Come and get it, I'm leaving anyway."

"Why leave Matey? Have a beer with us."

Louie's long lost smile returned, "Thanks", he said, "Make it a Schlitz."

The fellows ordered a couple of extra cans of beer and they all sat down around the table.

"Are you headed stateside?" one of them asked.

"No, not for months, "Louie said. Taking a called for long swig of beer.

"Wat'er ya doin ere then Matey?"

"The army is trying to make a clerk out of me," Louie explained.

"Fat chance. Say, where are you fellows headed?"

"Well, first we're flying to California and then by boat 'ome. Going 'ome from Korea we are. Twenty four stinking months in that 'ell 'ole. Twenty four rotten months and too many of them months we've been just sitting at the foot of Powder Top Hill while those blimey Chinks sat at the top and threw grenades at us. Ad'er zeroed in perfect with a wall of artillery and mortar fire and every time we tried to take that damn 'ill they'd slaughter us like bloody sheep, they would."

"What about the flanks?" Louie asked.

"Bloody mountain on one side of 'er and the Sea of Japan on the other."

"The valley in front of the 'ill is so bad that they call 'er Death Valley."

Since Louie had finished his beer he started to get up. "Hate to leave you fellows but I can't buy you a drink tonight."

"Sit down 'ere Yank. We've got two years pay and we're buying. Are there any girls around 'ere?"

"Not in camp, but they have a fine bunch in town."

"Wat are we waitin' for then Yank? Lead the way."

"But I wasn't going to town. I'm broke."

"You're not broke Yank. You've got us and we've got plenty of bloomin money. When we drink, you drink. When we get a girley you get a girley. Just call it our own little lend lease."

"Then you've got a partner. Just follow me fellows and I'll show you the sinful, wonderful Island of Eta Jima."

Louie began the tour with a trip to the town's leading Carabets. First stop was the Duckin Bar, the Bar Acme, Bar Stork, Bar New York and they were at the end of Cherry Street at the town's leading attraction which was ingeniously named Number One Beer Hall. It was formerly a Japanese Museum and when the Island was taken over by Americans some weird reasoning turned the hall into a Cabaret complete with girls, dancing and a floor show. It was there that the fellows got down to the serious business of refighting the battles of Korea. Louie told of his few months in combat and the

Australians went into detail describing their frustrating experience of spending two years without finally accomplishing their mission.

It was almost curfew time and Louie was feeling no pain when one of the Aussies explained how they thought the Brass in charge of the Korean War were all wrong in their approach to Powdertop Hill.

"If we could only make a small beachhead landing from the flank and a little to the rear, we could take that bloody 'ill. The Brass says it's impossible to make a small beach head attack. For some reason they say a beach head 'as to be all out. The 'ole bloomin Navy, at least a Division of Infantry. Air Strikes.

"We say that our platoon could do the job but they wouldn't let us give 'er a try. It doesn't seem right for them to be sendin' us 'ome without ever givin' it a go. Does it Matey?"

"You're damn right," Louie agreed. "It's a damn dirty shame and for two cents I'd tell you to go right ahead."

"That's good talk, Matey, we'd like nothing better. It's just a little matter of a boat and supplies, rifles and grenades. If we could only get those things we might give 'er a go."

"Well then let's get 'em." Everything seemed plausible to Louie at this stage. He was having trouble walking now.

"If you could get them, Matey, we'd be most grateful to you for the rest of our lives. Wouldn't we Mateys?"

"Aye, that we would," they all agreed.

"Then I'll talk to the fellows in the Unfit Outfit and see what we can do," Louie promised.

It was curfew time and Number One Beer Hall emptied out in a hurry. The men rushed back to camp and made it just in time. Louie went directly to the barracks and carefully woke each of the men with the exception of Corporal Tuttle. They held an emergency meeting in the latrine.

"I don't know how the rest of you men feel, but to me being a Personnel Clerk is about useless as trying to get Boots elected mayor of Atlanta, Georgia."

Boots winked at Louie and smiled broadly at the comparison.

Louie continued. "Now I admit I had a couple of beers tonight but I think I've come on a terrific opportunity. Tonight I met a swell bunch of Australian soldiers and they are going home. They've been in Korea for two years and for months now they haven't been able to capture Powder Top Hill. Now they've got this plan see. And it will work." Louie could hardly contain his excitement.

"All we have to do is get them a boat and some rifles and ammo and grenades and food and that's it. As for myself, if we can get all of that stuff then I'm going along. I just don't seem to be cut out for this clerkin' job and so this is my way to get back into the Infantry. What if I do get caught? It'd only mean couple of years in the stockade, and what the hell, I'd rather be in a stockade than be a damn personnel clerk. What do you say fellows?"

"Sounds like you've had quite a few beers," Charlie said.

"Maybe he has," Sammy agreed. "But that sounds pretty interesting to me. Where is this hill, Louie?"

"On the East Coast of Korea. We could make a little beach head landing and if we had a little luck we could take the hill with one good grenade attack. These Aussies have been working on this plan for months and no one will listen to them. You fellows don't have to go with them if you don't want to. That's just my idea, after all, it's a way out of this clerkin'."

"I'd like to get back to a man's work," Boots said. "You can count me in."

"Why not?" Frenchie agreed. "We're in trouble around here every day anyway, we might was well go for broke and do something useful."

"I could stand a little killing," Tom thought softly aloud.

Frank didn't like it. Sticking your neck out when it seemed so unnecessary. "It sounds too Gung-Ho to me. I've got no special desire to be a hero."

"You don't have to go," Louie said. "If your chicken Frank, just say so."

"I'll give you chicken Louie, I just said it sounds too Gung-Ho and I'm still the number one guy in my book."

"You can come or stay, make up your mind. Either you're in or you're out."

"I'm not staying here alone. What about you other guys?"

"You're not doing a stupid thing like that without taking me along," Charlie said. "Let's start planning this thing right now. We'll need a boat and that P.T. Boat that brought us from Kure will work just fine. It's fast with Twin Packard Engines, good long range and it makes a low silhouette. We can start saving up chow and this Island is loaded with rifles and ammo. All we have to do is a little midnight requisitioning. We'll split it up. Boots, you work on the boat and the gas. Louie, you get the food. I'll work on the ammo and rifles."

"Get grenades." Louie suggested. "Lots of grenades."

"And get me a machine gun," Sammy pleaded. "My own 30

caliber machine gun."

"Right. We'll set it up for a week from Thursday," Charlie suggested.

"That's the day before graduation," Louie reminded them.

"That's right. This'll be our Graduation Party."

"We're going to show those Chinks just how physically unfit we are," Boots said.

"We'll show the whole damn world," Louie agreed. He turned to Frank. "You in or out Frank, which is it?"

Frank smiled and hit Louie on the back. "In," he said.

"Then let's hit the sack and get some sleep," Louie said. "And remember, we've got to keep this thing quiet if we want to make it work. Tomorrow we start working. Operation Powder Top is on its way."

21

Craps

Ben had been seeing Yoshiko nearly every night. He would stop in for just a few minutes to see how she was coming along and was glad to see that she was up and around. The color was coming back into her face. It had been over a week since the operation and Ben was running out of excuses for seeing her. He'd convinced Yoshiko to write to her father and beg his forgiveness. He thought that perhaps if she could get back home, "Eversing might get to be Dai-Jobu (all right)." Somehow he felt responsible for her. He told her things would be all right and she seemed to be counting on him to make it happen. It was nearly 2100 hours when he stopped by her house. She was waiting on the small porch, which was nearly covered with G.I. shoes, when she saw him approaching her face lit up in a warm welcoming smile.

"I hope you come tonight, Ben-san. Tonight I very sorry. Two more day and then I must try to catch G.I. again."

The mere thought revolted him. "Did you hear from your father yet?"

Yoshiko looked very sad and shook her head, "No, Ben. I sink maybe he not read letter. Maybe just throw away. Papasan very angry, Yoshiko."

"Maybe tomorrow," Ben suggested.

"Yoshito hope so. Mamasan say never mind write letter. No go anyway, owe Mamasan too much money. Must catch many G.I. and pay Mamasan."

"How much you owe Mamasan?"

"Toxon (much). Maybe sirty founsand yen."

"Thirty thousand?" Ben exclaimed in surprise.

"Hi. Sirty fousand. Maybe 80 G.I. dollar."

"Oh, 80 dollars," Ben's surprise diminishing. "I was thinking thirty thousand dollars."

Yoshiko laughed. "Sirty thousand G.I. dollar you buy whole island of Eta Jima."

"Yeh, I guess so. Eighty bucks," Ben thought, it was a lot more than he had and the fact that payday was the next day didn't make that much difference. He was sending most of his money home to Ruth and all he would draw would be about $15. Eighty bucks was about as easy to get as the thirty thousand after all. Ben reached in his pocket and brought out the bar of soap he had bought for Yoshiko at the P.X.

She took it graciously and it was evident that her heart was overflowing with love and gratitude.

He sat with her on the porch a few moments and then headed back to camp. Tomorrow was another day, a busy day with class and the hustling of supplies.

"You come see Yoshiko tomorrow?" she almost pleaded.

Ben shrugged his shoulders. "Maybe." Somehow he just could not bring himself to say no.

After class the next day the men lined up for pay call. It was as Ben expected, $15. No more, no less. A lieutenant had a table set up nearby, soliciting donations for the Red Cross, but he might as well have stayed at Headquarters. He wasn't doing a bit of business.

As Ben returned to the barracks he spotted the inevitable Crap game starting up in the far corner of the barracks. He went over to his cot and sat down to write a long letter to Ruth. Nothing to write home, the same old grind, wished he could be home with her and the baby. He missed her very much. Nothing was new here, same old routine. He failed to mention his experience with Yoshiko, and also omitted any mention of the plans they were making with the Australians. No need to worry her, and hell, she would never understand that business with Yoshito. Best to keep it to himself. Maybe ten years from now, when he'd be back home and very happy with Ruth, he could tell her about it, but not now.

The letter finished and mailed, Ben wandered around the barracks which was quieting down. Some of the guys had already lost what little they had and some of the winners were headed for town as fast as they could. Though the noise had abated somewhat the crap game was still going strong, so Ben wandered over to watch the action. Ten dollar bills were rapidly changing hands. Some twenties too. Ben thought about what he could do with the size of that kitty.

The dice was bucking some of the shooters and after a few minutes Ben thought about Yoshiko again and the eighty dollars she needed. Ben could stand it no longer. He took the fifteen dollars out of his pocketbook and put five of it into the secret compartment of his wallet, as though he didn't trust himself. In fact he knew he couldn't but he'd try because he needed cigarette money. He got ten ones for his ten and started making side bets against the dice. He started out good and his hopes rose as he ran the ten up to twenty-five dollars, maybe he could make that eighty bucks for Yoshiko. His hopes were soon shot down as the dice changed moods and though it teased him on by letting him win a little, his whole ten dollars soon disappeared.

His last dollar had just disappeared into an eager hand when one of the men said, "It's your dice Ben, wanna try?"

Ben quickly reached into his wallet into the secret compartment and threw the five down as though there was a lot more where that came from. "Shoot five," he heard himself say.

Ben took the dice into his perspiring hands and rubbed them together and gave them a good blow for luck. "Come to papa," he cried as he snapped them against the footlocker. They rolled back out into the carefully folded blanket around which all the men were kneeling.

"Seven," someone yelled.

"Shoot the ten," Ben replied excitedly. He was quickly faded. Ben thought about Yoshiko, his need for cigarettes and a sense of guilt for what Ruthie might think of the chance he was taking. He grabbed the dice, blew hard again and sailed them up against the footlocker again. "Wow, seven again!"

"Let the twenty ride." He felt the anxiety building within as he blew and threw again. "Seven." What a relief! He dragged $15 from the pot, "Twenty five, this time boys." The guys knew that his luck was about to run out so it was quickly covered when he shot again, "Eleven," some amazed voices chorused.

"Shoot the fifty," Ben said nervously knowing that this could not go on much longer. It took maybe thirty seconds (nearly a lifetime in the mind of a hot craps shooter) but the fifty was soon covered.

Ben let them roll again. A groan went through the crowd. "Four."

"Little Joe," Ben called.

"Ten he don't make it!" one man chanted.

"Twenty he don't," another called out with conviction in his voice.

Ben took ten out of his pocket and covered the ten bet. Picked up the dice, rubbed them around in his hands, brought them up to his mouth and blew as near as he could to the way that had been bringing him such good luck. He seemed to be praying as it took a little longer before he let them roll.

"Four right back," they called. Ben picked up the hundred and twenty from the blanket. He put the hundred in his pocket and shot the twenty.

"Seven again."

He knew he had pushed lady luck to her high limit but couldn't resist trying again but hedged his bet a little by putting twenty in his pocket and shot the remaining twenty.

Again a quick roll. "Eight."

"Eighter from Decatur," Ben called.

"Craps," the gang cried as Ben passed the dice and walked jubilantly back to his cot to count his winnings. A hundred fifteen ahead. He hurridly dressed and headed for town. Everything was Dai-Jobu, mighty damn Dai-Jobu.

Yoshiko was sitting at her usual place on the tiny front porch and there were tears in her eyes as he joined her.

Ben spoke. "Konnichi-Wa (good evening)." He sat beside her as she shoved a few pairs of G.I. shoes aside. "Why are you crying?" he asked.

"Yoshiko veery, veery happy. Letter come today from Papasan. He say come home, Hayaku (Hurry up). He say he talk to man at teahouse and I get job back. Just no bring G.I."

"You're crying cause you're happy?"

"Also crying cause Yoshiko sad, veery sad. Tell Mamasan and she say Yoshiko no can go. She say she call police, have Yoshiko Awwwested."

"Why would she do that?"

"She say Yoshiko owe firty six fousand Yen and if no pay she call powice."

"That's a hundred dollars," Ben commented.

"I sink Mamasan tell lie I sink I owe her only firty fousand Yen. Maybe ony twenty fousand Yen. Not firty six fousand Yen."

"Let me talk to Mamasan," Ben offered and arose to go find her just as she came to the porch. She looked meaner and older than ever. "Mamasan," Ben started out not knowing the best way to approach the old lady, "Maybe I take Yoshiko and you no have to feed her any more."

Mamasan looked very suspicious. "Yoshiko owe me one hundred G.I. dollar," she growled.

"Never happen, Mamasan," Ben countered. "I give you ten thousand yen and you let her go. Yoshiko no good short-time girl. No catch G.I. She cost you money."

"I take firty fousand Yen," Mamasan bargained.

"I'll give you eighteen thousand yen and that's more than you should get," Ben spoke with conviction and as though to signify that was as far as he would go, put on his cap as he stepped off of the porch to indicate the haggling was over.

"You pay twenty fousand G.I. Twenty fousand Yen OK, G.I.?" The old lady was not about to give in too easily.

"You got a deal, Mamasan," Ben agreed as he pulled a wad of Yen from his pocket and peeled off twenty thousand Yen notes, glad that he had changed a hundred dollars into Yen before coming into town. Yoshiko began crying much harder now that she realized that Ben really had the money and actually had carried out the deal.

"Why are you crying now?" Ben knew the answer even as he asked.

"Yoshiko veery happy," she sobbed.

"That's good, I'm glad."

"But Yoshiko veery sad too. If Yoshiko go home to Papasan, then I don't see you any more."

"You're going home. I told you everything would turn out right and now it's happening. You're going home to your folks and be a good girl and lead a happy life. You can forget about me and the G.I.s, this Island and everything."

Yoshiko dabbed at the tears streaming from her big brown eyes as she gazed softly into Ben's big blue ones. "Maybe I forget everysing else Ben, buy I not forget you. Yoshiko never forget you. Yoshiko love you very much." The tears again started rolling across her soft cheeks.

"Now get your things packed, you're getting on a boat tonight."

Yoshiko smiled through her tears. "I don't want sings, I have here Ben, just toothbrush and bar of soap."

They walked arm in arm to the dock where Ben bought her a ticket. He gave her a fist full of Yen for train fare after she got off the boat. Just before she walked onto the boat she threw her arms around his neck and gave him a long slow, loving kiss. "How I say sank you Ben? Allegato such a small word. So big my sanks I cannot say."

Again she embraced him, but even more fervantly than before. On the lips, the cheeks, even pulled his head down to kiss him on the forehead. Tears came now from four eyes now as the big man's tears joined those of the petite little beauty. "Happy tears, veery happy tears," as they both tasted salty moisture as their lips met for the last time.

"Dai-Jobu tears," Ben almost sobbed. The boat whistle blew

to signal departure time. Ben quickly walked Yoshiko to the gangplank for one last squeeze of their hands over the gate. "Goodbye Yoshiko."

"Saynara, Bensan," she sobbed, turned and ran quickly up the plank just before it was raised.

"Saynara," Ben repeated savoring the soft sound of her last words. He stood there a long time waiting until the boat disappeared in the darkness.

He turned to walk slowly back into town with a heavy heart and very mixed emotions. He stuck his hands in his pockets as though they were too heavy to carry any other way. One hand jammed into the few Yen left. He changed directions and headed for the Bar Swan and got drunk.

A few days later he walked down Cherry Street the girls no longer invited him to their house. Instead they bowed with respect and admiration, "Konnichi-Wa Ben-chan (Good evening, Ben)."

"Hai--before Ben-san but now very honorable and special person. Now we call you Ben-Chan."

Word travels fast on a small island and Ben was now recognized as a very special person among the girls of Eta Jima. He felt really good about it, he had set a butterfly free.

Tom Gomez took his pay and carefully laid it in a series of small piles of his cot. He had $45 after paying his debts and setting aside $15 for cigarettes, shaving cream, blades and other necessary items. That left $30 and Tom wanted to send his folks some souvineers. He also wanted to rent a bicycle and make a complete tour of the island. It was funny. Tom had taken his money and made the little piles so many times and yet it never seemed to work. He had to force himself to buy the things he had to have before he went into town or he knew he would never get them. He picked up his money and went directly to the P.X., made his purchases and converted the rest to Yen. After locking his things in his footlocker, he headed for the village.

His mind made up, he would buy the souvineers for his folks and send them right out to his folks and when that was done he would rent that bicycle and take that ride around the island. "It's so damn simple," he tried to persuade himself. "Why can't I just go do it?"

Tom walked through the gate and turned down Cherry Street aiming for the New York Gift Store. He'd tried this once before and was diverted by the joyful sounds coming out of the Tiger Bar which was just two doors from the gift shop. Another time he had made it only as far as the Bar Clover which was the first Cabaret from the base gate. This time he made it as far as the Bar Pearl which was just next door to the gift shop.

One beer wouldn't hurt, he told himself. Just like he always told himself, then he'd buy the things for his folks and rent the bicycle. That's what he told himself, he knew he was lying.

As always one beer led to two, then three, then four and then you had to buy a round to pay back someone that had bought you one. Tom drank continously on into the night, he staggered back into camp. No bike ride, no souvineers this month.

P.F.C. Tom Gomez was a troubled man. God how he hoped he might have just one more chance to prove himself in combat. He simply could not live with himself, not sober, he couldn't.

When he awoke the next morning he felt angry with himself and wondered why he couldn't do a simple thing like make a few purchases, rent a bike and take that tour? It didn't make sense and yet it was the story of his life. Every time he had one beer he had to have another. When he got his hands on a bottle of whiskey he had to finish it as soon as possible. "What in the hell is wrong with me?" he would often ask himself. "When am I going to learn how to drink?"

Tom didn't know it, but he wouldn't have time to worry about the problem for long. From then on the men were busy every moment, either attending classes or working on their own secret project. So engrossed, in fact, that Tom didn't have time to get drunk again.

22

The Plot Thickens

Louie wasted no time the following morning locating his ten Aussie drinking buddies.

"Well fellows, we're lining up a boating expodition just like you suggested last night."

"Yer kiddin', Yank."

"No, I'm not kiddin. You fellows want to make a beachhead invasion, so we'll make a beachhead invasion."

"'e's off is bloomin rocker, I think," the Aussie said.

"Now just a minute," Louie said. "You guys wanted a chance to take Powdertop Hill and a bunch of us fellows would like to see a little excitement too and so we've decided to go with you. It's all set for a week from Thursday. We'll get the boat and everything we need. You fellows just stick around 'til then and we'll be on our way. Now I want you boys to work up some maps for us. You can start planning the trip right from this Island. We figure we'll go in just before dawn."

"By God, I think e's leveling with us."

"Of course I'm leveling. When the American Infantry sets out to do something, it gets done. Now we don't officially represent the American Infantry but we plan on representing them on our own. Just get those maps worked out and keep this thing quiet. We'll take care of everything else."

"'Ey Bobbie, 'ow we going to stay on this island 'til a week from Tuesday?"

"We'll stay, Matey, we'll just have to stall around that long."

Louie rushed to class and just barely made it into the classroom on time. He'd told Tuttle he had personal business to take care of at the office and Tuttle had believed him. The fellows just didn't seem to be their usual selves that morning. Everyone seemed to be cooperative. Too cooperative perhaps. It was as if they had lost their old stuff. No bickering, no back talk. They just seemed to want to get it over with without any delays. They avoided him all day.

The men kept gathering in little groups discussing some major project.

Whenever Tuttle would try to get near them they'd start talking about the weather or Military Courtesy. Something big was cooking. He could smell it but he just couldn't find out what.

The following day was more of the same. The men obeyed his every order without hesitation. They cleaned up around their cots, shined their shoes and for some unknown reason none of them were going to town. They were running here and there about the camp every free moment they had.

The weekend was the same procedure. Whatever it was they were planning was certainly being very carefully kept a secret. The men appeared happier too, much, much happier, and yet at times they looked very serious. He had run into two of the men in the Library reading books on of all things, navigation. He had even imagined he had seen Louie stuffing a peck of potatoes into his wall locker. Or had he imagined it?

A whole week passed. The men seemed to be getting more and more excitable every day. He thought about talking with Captain Thompson and yet what was there to tell him? The men were merely cooperating with him and with the Army. Was there anything wrong with this? Knowing these fellows, yes plenty. They were up to something. Something big, but what? When? Where? How? This was a deep, dark, hidden secret. Tuttle decided to do a little investigating before he went to the Captain. After all, the Captain wasn't very nice to him since that deal with the Provost Marshall. He felt the best thing to do was just to stick around his room and keep his eyes and ears open.

Tuttle laid on his cot pretending to be reading a book when Boots came running into the barracks. He spotted Louie and called him over to the corner of the room.

"We've got it made, Louie. I've been hanging around the dock and I talked one of the swabbies into giving me an ignition key. It cost me two-fifths of Canadian Club, but now we've got a key. I told him I was a key collector and I just had to have a boat key for my collection. I don't suppose he believed me but for two-fifths he didn't care what I wanted the key for. He had several spares and it didn't matter to him. I found out they keep the boat gassed up and ready to go in case they get a special night call."

"Those swabbies are sure nice guys," Boots continued. "They showed me how to start the boat and how to run it and everything. Even showed me where they store their gasoline. There are plenty of full fuel cans there and we can really load up before we take off. They don't have a guard either. After all, who would dare to steal a boat from the United States Navy?"

"Ya, who would dare?" Louie laughed.

"How you coming on the food?" Boots asked.

"I've got it made," Louie replied. "A cook I knew in Korea is teaching at the Cook School and he's got it all set. All the supplies we need. He'll even come along and cook if we want him."

"I guess we've got room," Boots decided. "After all, this deal will take a couple of days and we can't starve. Are you sure you can trust him?"

"All I can say is that I ate his cookin' for three months and I'm still alive."

"Good enough," Boots smiled. "Tell him to have the food and himself ready for Thursday night."

About 2300 Charlie came walking into the barracks. He looked exhausted. His uniform was dirty and soaked with sweat. He nudged Boots and Louie who were sleeping and motioned for them to join him in the latrine.

"Man, oh Man, what a raid. We hustled enough stuff to take Powder Top, Old Baldy, Heartbreak and Pork Chop Hill thrown in," Charlie explained. "We got a machine gun, 25 carbine automatic rifles, six 45s and plenty of ammo for everybody."

"What about grenades?" Louie asked.

"We've got enough grenades to win a war. Helments too, and ammo belts, canteens, bayonettes, first aid kits and even a mortar with shells. Everything we could possibly need for a hot fast patrol raid. Now, if you fellows can feed us and get us there then we've got it made."

"Then we've got it made. Louie's got the food all set and I've got the boat lined up."

"And those Australians have the maps all ready," Louie added. "They've got that trip mapped out so well that we can't possibly miss it."

"Then tomorrow night we go," Charlie said. "Let's set it up for 2200. Pass the word to everyone and tell them to keep it quiet. Louie, you pass the word to the Aussies, and may the Good Lord take a liking to us."

"Amen brother," the two men replied.

They all walked back into the barracks and climbed into their sacks. Corporal Tuttle, who was sleeping with one eye opened watched them and then spent the rest of the night wondering what was about to happen.

23

D-Day

Thursday morning was just like any other morning had been lately. The fellows treated Tuttle just as if he was a real Corporal. The tests were given and all of the men came through with flying colors. They were respectful and obedient. Something was seriously wrong. Tuttle could just sense that all hell was going to break loose and yet there was nothing he could do. He had kept his eyes and ears open and yet he had discovered nothing. Whatever it was had to do with boats and potatoes. Beyond that he was at a loss. Tuttle walked up to Charlie on their first smoke break and tried to get a little information.

"I suppose that since this is the last day and seeing that we graduate tomorrow, you men will be going to town to blow off a little steam tonight," Tuttle said.

"I don't know."

"Aren't you fellows going to have a party?" Tuttle asked.

"We haven't given it much thought," Charlie replied.

"Oh, I thought that maybe it was a party that you fellows had been working so hard on the last few weeks."

"Nope," Charlie said, walking away and signalling for Louie to join him.

"Beautiful day isn't it?" Charlie asked.

"Superb."

"Don't you think it's a lovely day, Corporal?"

"Uh, Yea," Tuttle was baffled. He'd be glad when graduation was over, then he'd be transferred away from these screwy fellows. He never did understand what was going on in their heads. He'd sure like to know what it was they were working on this time, but they just weren't talking.

The men seemed in a happy and excited mood as they marched back to their quarters after classes that evening. When they arrived in the barracks each man sat down and wrote a letter home. Some wrote several. These fellows were dead serious. They didn't seem to be the same old hell-raising gang that had given him so many sleepless nights. They seemed to have lost the feeling that they had to fight the Army and its regulations. "Maybe the Army had taught them something at this school besides how to be clerks," he thought hopefully. Maybe they were learning real Leadership School kind of soldiering. Maybe...no, not those guys, who was he kidding? They were up to something and he decided to stick around the barracks and see if he could find out what.

At 2100 Tuttle was still sitting on his cot pretending to read his book.

"Aren't you going to town Tuttle?" Frank asked.

"Not tonight," Tuttle replied. "I'm just going to lay around and take it easy."

"Why don't you look up that American Army Civilian worker?" Louie asked.

"How did he know about her?" Tuttle wondered. Hell with their Intelligence System they probably had movies of the whole thing.

"I'm just staying here tonight," Tuttle replied.

Frank called Frenchie and Boots over to the corner.

"We've got to get rid of him before we leave. Suppose we just tie him up and gag him. It'll be a couple of hours before they find him and that's all the time we need. Let's get with it fellows."

Boots walked slowly towards Tuttle's cot.

Frenchie put a pillow case over Tuttle's mouth as Boots tied his hands and feet securely. They carried him over to the far corner of the barracks and tied him to the foot of the cot. He couldn't possibly get loose.

"Well fellows," Charlie announced. "It's about that time. Let's get with it, we've got quite an evening ahead of us."

The men split up and walked separately to the dock. When Frank arrived the others were already there. Louie had several fellows helping to load the food into the boat and Charlie was carrying crates full of ammunition and hand grenades aboard. Boots was up near the wheel and the Aussies who weren't helping with the loading were busy with Boots studying the maps. The gasoline had been loaded and there was plenty for the trip.

Meanwhile back at the camp, Sgt. Riley was walking down the long hallway outside the barracks room when he heard a muffled cry from inside. He looked in and saw nothing and started to leave when he heard the cry once again.

He followed the sound to the back of the room and there in the far corner of the barracks on the floor he found Corporal Tuttle tied hand and feet to a cot, with a gag in his mouth.

Quickly Riley pulled the gag off Tuttle's mouth.

"Those idiots are going to get themselves killed, Sergeant. We've got to stop them," Corporal Tuttle cried out excitedly.

"Now slow down Tuttle," Sergeant Riley said. "What are you talking about?"

"The class," Tuttle said. "The whole class. They are stealing a boat and making their own beach-head attack on North Korea."

"What boat?" Riley asked.

"I don't know," Corporal Tuttle explained. "Untie me. We've got to tell the Captain and stop them."

Sergeant Riley thought about it just an instant and then he reached down and stuffed the gag back in Tuttle's mouth.

"Untie you, Hell," he said and he turned and broke into a full run out of the barracks and out of camp on down the road toward the dock.

In a matter of about two minutes the boat was loaded and the lines were loosened. Boots started the engines and everyone took a seat. The last line was thrown ashore and just as Boots was about to pull out he heard a voice and saw someone running down the dock towards the boat.

"It's Sergeant Riley," Louie yelled. "Get going fast."

"Hold it! Hold it!" Sergeant Riley screamed.

"Get going," Louie called and Boots immediately raced the powerful engines and the boat quickly raced away from the dock. At that instant, Sergeant Riley leaped through the air and landed on the rear deck of the boat.

"Thank God I made it," Riley said as he rubbed his leg which had landed on a gasoline can. "I heard what you fellows are up to and it sounds great to me," Sergeant Riley continued. "I think Captain Thompson is off his rocker. His wife wrote him that she was going to divorce him. She's going with a guy in the navy, a common seaman, no rank or anything but she's throwin the Captain over for this guy. He just sits at his desk and shines those damn Captain's bars of his and figures out ways to give everybody a hard time. Another day with that misplaced civilian bastard they call a Captain and I'm liable to do something that will put me in the stockade for life. At least this way it's for something worthwhile."

"How much do you know about what we're doing?" Louie asked.

"I know you're going to Korea," the Sergeant replied.

"Then we might as well fill you in on the whole thing."

The more Riley heard about the plan the better he liked it. The men passed out supplies and each man cleaned and readied his weapon. Grenades and helmets were issued. Several times the maps were laid out on deck and the plan was carefully reviewed and rereviewed. The Australians studied their new rifles religiously, taking them apart again and again. They looked over the grenades and practice pulling pins and replacing them.

The sea was quiet, almost glass smooth and the moonlight made the trip an almost enjoyable one. The powerful P.T. Boat raced toward their objective at top speed. As the boat sped through the Straits near Moji, Louie and his cooking friend had set out a half dozen hibachis on the deck and on the hot white coals they were carefully preparing hamburgers for a midnight snack. Once through the Straits, the boat headed north and then northwest. The Sea of Japan was calm and quiet and the men watched the lights along the Northern coast of Japan. Soon the lights were gone. They were making wonderful time.

Boots were keeping careful tabs on the boat's engines and Tom Gomez walked up to where Boots was standing.

It was obvious that P.F.C. Tom Gomez was a troubled man. He tried to act casual, as he spoke to Boots, but his voice gave him away. "Can I talk to you Boots?" he asked.

Boots smiled and replied, "Sure man, what's up?"

"Well," Tom said hesitantly. "You saw a lot of combat?"

"A little," Boots admitted.

"Well I was just wondering," Tom continued. "Well, did you ever feel like running away when people were falling dead all around you?"

Boots laughed. "You're damn right I did."

"Well what did you do?" Tom asked.

"I just forced myself to run toward the enemy instead of away. You just have to take a deep breath and act crazy, that's all."

Tom smiled a faint smile. "You really felt like running away?" he asked.

"Of course," Boots said. "Everybody feels that way. It's a natural instinct to want to run away from death."

"Thanks," Tom said.

"No sweat," Boots said and he put his arm around Tom and gave him a hug. "We are going to do just fine in this battle. Just stick with me and we'll do all right."

Now Korea stood quietly to their left. Ulsan, Yongdok, Chukpyon, Samchok, then Kangnung, Yangyany and now they were nearing Kosong. The men had been sleeping in shifts and now they were all awake and filling up on their last cup of coffee. Dawn was just coming up as their boat drifted to the shore, right on time, right on target.

Five hundred yards to go. Charlie now addressed the men as a unit. "When we hit that beach, start running. We may draw enemy fire right away. Spread out and head for the hill. If you see a Chink, then kill him with your knife, if you can. We don't want to fire a weapon until we're up the hill. This is it men! The Unfit Outfit is back in the Infantry. God help us. God give us the luck and strength to see it through."

"Amen," the men whispered in unison.

"Now Go!" Charlie yelled.

24

Doing It

Dawn broke at 0552 and at that instant the men waded ashore, their bayonets fixed. Each step brought out a greater supply of a combat soldier's greatest asset--fear. Until now it had been a happy, carefree adventure. The hustling of supplies, the planning, the secrecy. Now the lark part was over, but the combat soldier has been trained not to think about the personal consequences, winning is the only thing. An individual becomes a small part, a perfectly dependable working part of something bigger. They now faced the grim business of killing, of protecting each other while trying to stay alive.

Fear becomes an alley if it is not wild and uncontrolled, but strengthening. It puts the well-trained and disciplined fighter in an altered state of consciousness where his perceptions are enhanced. He automatically becomes aware of sounds, movements otherwise ignored. Fear provides that something extra in the blood that allowed you to run 100 yards farther, carrying a heavy pack, then would ordinarily be possible.

Bravery was always there in varying amounts, but it was fear and extensive training that took you up the hill and pulled off the rounds of your M-1 Rifle or helped you throw the grenade that knocked out machine gun positions. Fear was what gave you that extra energy and the needed caution and intuition that kept you alive to do the job.

They had crawled inland only a hundred yards when they received another valuable asset to help them on their mission--hate. Charlie spotted it first, "The bastards. The dirty little yellow bastards," he whispered so the others could see what he was pointing at. An Australian soldier was tied to a tree. He was long dead, just sagging against the ropes, a trail of dried blood ended in a pool at his feet. On the tree, where his head had been before being blown away, was the outline of a target.

"They used him for target practice," Frank commented in

credously.

They paused and took in the terrible scene for a full moment, each man building a heart full of hatred. Hatred that would cause a fighting man's body to keep right on fighting though mortally wounded. They had felt it before, but somehow the weeks in the hospital and school had dimmed their memory of what the fighting was all about. The sight of that dead Australian would cost the Chinese far more than they ever got out of it. Once again the real, overall purpose of their mission became worthwhile.

Now they again started moving forward and after another hundred yards or so, Sergeant Riley signalled them down and to be quiet. They settled into the ground like shadows, trying to make sure there was no two pieces of equipment clanging against each other.

They did not have long to wait when they heard the casual footsteps of a guard walking his post. Perhaps he was thinking of his girlfriend or family back home. He apparently believed that he was a long way from danger so he did not hurry when he turned to investigate the slight noise Sergeant Riley made as he leaped up behind him. Riley's swift bayonet movements ended the guards thoughts forever.

Quickly the men dragged the dead soldier under the brush and at Riley's signal they started moving forward again. When they reached the base of the hill everything was quiet. They took a moment to calm their breathing, ready their grenades, say a prayer perhaps and begin the long dangerous climb up the hill.

"We'll blow their blooming arses off this time, eh, Bobbies?" an Australian said quietly to himself as much as to anyone in particular. "We'll make it to the top this 'ere time."

Everyone was hoping he was right, but nobody answered. They were too busy trying to stay quiet and close to the ground as they moved up the hill. They were prepared for and expecting opposition. Each step up that hill was one step closer to action. Suddenly they heard voices. Chinese. Riley cautioned them to be still. They didn't need a second signal. The voices soon faded away in the distance. The tone of the voices did not indicate any alarm. Still the hardest half, the most dangerous part of the hill lay ahead.

Now, finally, a mere 20 yards to go. Riley took two grenades off his belt and signalled to the men to prepare for the assault. All hearts were beating faster, perspiration was flowing freely in their palms, more was running down their backs. The ground beneath their feet was as dry as the inside of their mouths. The ground had been reduced to the consistancy of flour from the continuous artillery pounding. They crawled up to just below the rim of the hill and stopped for last minute physical, emotional and spiritual preparations. Everything was still, too still. Riley turned both ways, looking each man in the eye until he received a nod, a wink or a wave of a doubled up fist to indicate readiness.

The men waited silently until Riley waved, wildly screaming, "Get them men!"

The men threw their grenades over the top and following the explosions they went over themselves. They would throw at anything that looked like a target and drop to the ground until the blast was over, jump up and run forward again. They threw and hit the ground, jump up, run forward, throw another and hit the ground.

Sammy quickly set up his machine gun on top of a blown out bunker. It was ideal. He could shoot over the heads of his buddies and still be somewhat protected himself. He was blazing away in a matter of seconds. Above the din of the grenades and automatic rifle fire you could hear him yell, "Jackpot." Another burst. "Jackpot." Every time he let off a burst, a jackpot of shells came spurting out and dead Chinese were falling everywhere.

Boots quickly ran to cover the right flank, Tom Gomez hung in close beside him to take care of anything Boots didn't see. Suddenly Tom yelled, "Over there!" They both hit the bottom of a artillery crater and swiveled their attention to a Chinese machine gun that was just starting to spit death out its snout. The rounds were hitting the edge of the crater and throwing dirt all over them. They were pinned down in very cramped quarters. That gun would soon have the dirt dug away enough that the slugs would no longer go pinging off into space but would be coming into their shallow pit.

Boots looked through the flying dirt at Tom, who gave a brief smile back in thanks for the warning that saved him. He pulled a grenade off his belt for Boots to see, pointed at himself to let Boots know what he was about to do.

He had seen the exact location of the machine gun nest while Boots only had a brief warning from Tom that it was coming into action. Tom pulled the pin as a burst of gunfire stopped coming their way. He let go of the little handle that indicated it was safe as long as it held close to the body of the grenade. The grenade was designed to go off a few seconds after that lever swung out. That did not mean that you could bet your life it would wait, after all it was manufacturered by the lowest bidder, some company that offered to make them cheaper than anyone else.

Tom counted beneath his breath "One thousand one, one thousand two, one thousand three, one thousand four," then as though casually preparing to toss a baseball overhand to a friend he raised slightly, lobbed the grenade into the trench holding the machine gun where it fell to the ground. One of the Chinese picked it up to throw it back out before it exploded, but time had run out. It exploded instantly. Tom waited a few seconds trying to determine if the grenade had carried out its intended purpose. He took a chance, jumped out of his tiny hole and raced to where it had landed and dropped into the trench. Not a movement from the four dead Chinese laying there. Tom signaled Boots that it was OK and the two buddies advanced on up the slope.

Burp guns fired over on the left flank as surprised Chinese fell dead sometime almost at the feet of the charging, fast firing Aussies.

Riley crawled over to an underground bunker and threw in a grenade. The murderous explosion took care of any Chinese that might be hiding inside. The explosion was followed by deathly silence inside the bunker as well as outside. Over fifty Chinese bodies were strewn over the landscape, some bodies still in one piece, more were not. Hand grenades are deadly efficient, but they tend to leave a great mess around afterwards. They are the close range, heavy artillery a combat soldier can carry on his belt. The men looked cautiously around, there was no other sign of the Chinese around the hill. The hill was theirs and they'd suffered only a few minor wounds.

Ben, Frank, Boots, Sammy and Frenchie were jubilant, they had made it. They were real men again. They'd proved that they were fit for any man's army. They felt the real joy of victory that can only come to those that have looked death eye to eye and survived. They ran towards each other to exchange handshakes that only victors could appreciate or participate in. The Australians started making contact by radio with their comrades at the outposts down in Death Valley.

Suddenly the men noticed a movement from a bloody Chinese body laying a few feet away. The men realized that the man's last movement was to toss one of his own burning grenades into their midst. Fear came back to their assistance in an instant. Ben's rifle fired from the crook of his arm where it had been cradled. It caught the Chink with a volley that stopped him--dead. The men jumped away, literally flying in different directions in search of cover that was not there. Each expecting to feel the sting of hot steel ripping at their bodies just as they had seen the dismembered, shredded bodies of the Chinese.

The grenade exploded with a muffled roar. Each man checked his senses to see if the body and head were still intact. One by one the men got up as the echo of the explosion rang in their ears. Each was amazed that he was still alive. All except Frank Tucker. When Frank saw the grenade he instinctively knew that there was no time to get it and throw it out of danger. There was only time for one thing and it was the one useful thing that Frank Tucker was put on this earth to do. He knew that it was Gung-Ho and brave and stupid and decent. He knew that when you did things like that you lost your girlfriend and your buddies. But in that flashing second he knew exactly where his priorities stood. He did not hesitate a second, he threw his body over the grenade just as it exploded. He did the greatest thing a man can do and he can do it only once. He gave his life for his buddies. Frank Tucker was dead.

Within a few minutes a squad of Aussies arrived in response to signals the men had sent. They too were overjoyed to learn that the hill was theirs.

"The Unfit Outfit has proven that we're real men!" Louie exclaimed. "Especially Frank Tucker!"

Louie took Frank's rifle and stuck it bayonet first, into the ground and put Frank's helment on top of the rifle butt. The man came to attention and saluted as a final tribute to a real hero, Frank Tucker.

There was a lump in Louie's throat and his eyes were wet as he removed Frank's personal belongings to be sent back to his folks. He stood up, took one last look at his friend lying on the ground. "Let's get the hell out of here!" he said with a strained voice.

Without their artillery observers on top of Powdertop Hill, the Communists' guns could not operate effectively. By the time they could begin firing again the Aussies had brought forward enough men to defend the hill without any further attack.

In the confusion that followed the men returned to the boat and set a direct course for Eta Jima. Once away from shore they began to recover from the terrific strain brought on by their attack.

"We did it just like we planned," Boots exclaimed excitedly. "We did it with only one casualty, thank God. That grenade would have got us all if it had not been for Frank."

"I don't give a damn if they lock me up for the rest of my life. It was worth it. Just think, a bunch of 'B' profiles and we took that hill with no help from the Navy, no help from the Air Force and no help from the Army," Louie added. "And God bless those Australians, thanks to them guys I feel like a real man again!"

The cook had stayed on the boat to guard it but after they boarded for the jubilant return trip he outdid any previous meal. Steaks broiled on the hibachis and everyone ate to his heart's content. The spirits were higher that night than any time since they were wounded months before.

Sergeant Riley was enthusiastic. "I've always wanted to go on an attack like that. Being a Medic was all right, but after I got hit I had that awful feeling I'd never be able to fight back. Now I figure I'm about even. From here on out, I don't give a damn what the Army does with me. Anything will be better than sitting next to that misplaced civilian asshole they call a Captain."

Everyone was in high spirits, the Aussies were so thrilled and proud that they just kept hitting each other on the back and remarking in their own version of the English language, "Hy'd say we did hit all right, Ey, Bobbies? Right good show. Now let's 'ave a little nip to celebrate, 'ey?"

Tom Gomez was the only one to pass up the Canadian Club Whiskey the Aussies had brought on board in anticipation of winning. Tom looked and acted like an entirely different person. There was a wide, confident smile on his face. He was standing taller than he had in years. "No, Sir!" he exclaimed when offered the bottle. "I don't need that stuff anymore."

Privately Tom thanked Boots for his support and he was brushed off with a friendly, "No sweat, Man! I'd be happy to have you fighting or living by my side anytime."

As the boat docked at Eta Jima the case of Canadian Club was rapidly having its effect on the elated bunch and they were singing at the top of their voices, "The Bonnie Banks of Lochloma."

They kept right on singing when Captain Thompson appeared on the dock with Corporal Tuttle running along beside him like a well-trained little puppy.

Even when a squad of M.P.s appeared, they continued their boisterous singing. They kept right on repeating the song as they tied up the boat and walked into the waiting arms of the M.P.s.

"I'm going to Court Martial every single man that was on that boat," the Captain roared, his face red with anger. "Every damn one of you. What in the hell is the matter with you idiots? What gave you guys the idea you could steal a government boat and go traipsing off on a South Sea cruise? I'm going to get you for desertion, stealing everything from food to ammunition, the gas and everything." He seemed to be just getting warmed up as he went on with his roaring lecture. "You guys want a vacation. You're sure as hell going to get one. The Inspector General won't save your asses this time. I knew you bastards were up to something, things were too damn quiet. I didn't think you would go this far though. This time you went too damn far." Turning to the M.P.s he continued, "Put every damn one of them in the stockade. I'll General Court Martial every one of them."

Thompson started hollering at the Sergeant as he was marched by, "Sergeant Riley, I'm surprised at you. Really surprised. What in the world ever possessed you to go with these men?"

Riley smiled, his big Irish lopsided drunken smile, "Went fer the ride, is all."

"Where did you go?"

"Jus' around thas all. We got tired of the women on this here island and so we thought we'd try a couple of other spots. Man, the women really go for that hot rod boat, it's just like riding down the beach in a Cadillac convertible," Riley said pointing at the boat.

Thompson turned to the M.P.s, "Lock him up with the rest of those bums."

The M.P.s escorted the slightly inebriated men from the dock. Only the Captain and Tuttle remained, standing there in perplexed silence. For once Tuttle knew he better keep his mouth shut.

"Corporal."

"Yes, Sir."

"Corporal, how would you like to be my new First Sergeant?"

"I'd love that, Sir, I'm sure I can do the job, Sir."

"Corporal, I know a born leader when I see one. I am sure that I can depend on you to carry out my orders better than the last Sergeant I had. I'm sure I won't be disappointed in you."

25

Ultimate Punishment

It was early when the guards woke the men. They had to pay now for the heavy drinking they had done on the boat. Their throats were sore from the many choruses of Lochloma. Their muscles were sore from the previous day's excursion and although they were deeply mournful over Frank's death, still they were satisfied and proud of their accomplishment. The guards assigned the men striped prisoner's fatigues and then they were escorted to breakfast.

Meanwhile, Captain Thompson was rushing around the base making arrangements for the General Court Martials. The morning boat from Kure arrived early and, instead of the usual compliment of a few officers and enlisted men, the boat was jammed with Generals and Colonels. Several Australian Officers also were aboard. Captain Thompson was quickly summoned to the Base Commandant's Office. As he entered the office he was greeted by a General.

"Where is the Unfit Outfit, Captain?"

"The Unfit Outfit?" Captain Thompson stammered.

"That's right, the class."

"What class do you mean, General?"

"I mean the Unfit Outfit!" the General roared. "I understand that's what they call themselves."

"Do you know who he means Tuttle?" the Captain asked. Tuttle was standing near the doorway to the office, as the Captain had ordered.

"I guess the General means the fellows from our Personnel Management Class, Captain," Tuttle suggested.

"Oh No," Captain Thompson sighed, his knees grew weak, he braced himself as best he could and asked, "Tell me General, what did they do? Did they get into trouble with the women on one of those other islands? Did they kill the sacred deer at Miyajima? Did they rob a distillery on the mainland? Tell me General, what did they do?"

The General ignored the Captain and looked very disturbed, "I asked you where they were, Captain."

Captain Thompson's confidence returned. "In the Stockade, General. I've already had them locked up." He smiled now, quite proud of his excellent handling.

"Locked them up," the General roared. "You locked them up?" Blood rushed to his face and he took a deep breath trying to control himself. "Release them immediately. IMMEDIATELY, do you understand? And when they are rested, have them report to this office."

"Yes Sir, General Sir," the Captain stammered. "I'll do it immediately."

In a few moments the men were given back their regular uniforms and ordered to report to the Captain's office.

The men assembled outside the Stockade and Sergeant Riley called them to attention. With proud precision the men marched across the field and down the road to the Captain's office. Sharp? None sharper. They were Infantry soldiers. To hell with the Captain and the whole damn army. Nothing second class about them, their heads were held high, chest out, guts in, to hell with the Captain, whatever he wanted didn't bother them now. They could take anything, now that they had proved they were men again.

They waited outside the office while Sergeant Riley went in and reported. The Captain quickly came out in the hallway and addressed the men.

"You are to report to the Base Commander's Office as soon as you have made yourselves presentable and feel sufficiently rested. Is that understood?" Captain Thompson asked.

"Yes Sir," Sergeant Riley snapped. He called the men to attention and saluted. The men were dismissed and headed for the barracks.

"What in the hell is this?" Louie asked. "When we feel rested. Boy I've heard a lot of nutty orders but I never heard one like that."

"That is what is known as the Kid Glove Treatment, Louie," Sergeant Riley explained. "That's the Army's way of being polite to us. It looks like we are now V.I.P.s."

"Does it mean we get to rest up?" Charlie asked.

"Hell no," Riley explained. "All it means is that we better get the hell over there as soon as we can. They just said it in a polite way."

The men quickly shaved and showered and after hitting their boots a couple of good licks they donned their Class A uniforms, shined up their brass, put on their Combat Infantry Badges and headed for the Commander's office.

For the following four hours the men were put through a constant barrage of questioning. Both American and Australian Officers asked about every phase of their operation. "Where did they get the plan?" "How did they get the weapons?" "Who led the attack?" "How did Frank Tucker die?" "Why did they do such an incredible thing?" There was no doubting that the Generals were greatly impressed. They treated the men with courtesy and respect. They roared in laughter as Frenchie described how Corporal Tuttle was put out of action. They winked slyly as Charlie described his midnight requisitioning of Munitions. They choked with deep respect as the men described Frank Tucker's heroic death. On and on, question after question and finally a Three Star General addressed the men.

"And I suppose that Sergeant Riley was in charge of the entire operation?"

"No sir," Ben explained. "He came in on the deal at the last moment. We are all equally responsible."

"Well, you seem to be the spokesman," a General said.

"We all take full responsibility equally," Frenchie said.

"Well, just the same you need a spokesman and we're choosing Ben for the job."

"That's fine with us," the men agreed. "Only thing, if you're passing out punishment, we all will share it equally."

Ben was ordered into the next room. The men sat silently waiting to see what would happen next. Time passed slowly now. After what seemed like hours Ben came through the door.

"I just talked to General Eisenhower on the phone. The President himself. He wants to meet us in Washington. Wants to talk about our beachhead, you know he had a lot to do with a beachhead himself once. We're all going Stateside right away. Ike explained that since we broke so many rules and regulations that we have to be punished but that he is real proud of what we did."

"YA HOOO!" the roar went out. "STATESIDE!"

"I wonder what kind of punishment we'll get," Boots said.

The General appeared in the doorway. "I can answer that right now, and it might be kind of rough but let's face it, we can't very well commend you men for breaking all those regulations."

"I guess you're right, General," Ben said. "Well, General, what's the bad news?"

A big smile filled the General's face. "We're flunking you men out of Personnel Management School," he said.

The men roared with joy. With a failure from Personnel Management School on their records they would never be placed in clerk's jobs.

"Now get your things cleared up here fellows, you're all leaving for Toyko on the morning train and from there you'll fly to Washington."

The men headed out of the office and Charlie stayed behind the talk to the General for a few minutes.

Captain Thompson was only too happy to give the men passes for the rest of the day. There was a dirty rumor going around that he and Tuttle were being transferred to Korea for a little change in duties.

Sammy headed straight for the Pachinko Parlor. There wasn't much time left for him to make his killing.

Ben went to the Mail Room hoping to get a letter from Ruth. Instead of one letter there were two. One bore a Japanese Stamp and the postmark said Kokura, Japan. It was from Yoshiko. Ben glanced at both letters and then instinctively opened the one from Yoshiko first. It was very difficult to read. Yoshiko certainly couldn't write English but the sheer simplicity of the letter made it all the more meaningful. "We Japanese people say little of love," he read. "My people marry by family arrangement and after marriage then sometime come love. Sometime never come love. Yoshiko very, very lucky for she feel great, great love. Yoshiko have very big love for you, Bensan. Maybe Yoshiko never see you again, but know in heart that she love you for all time. You make Yoshiko very Happiness. I hope you very happiness too. Maybe you get this letter before go Stateside. If you ever lonely or sad, Bensan, you think about Yoshiko because I, all time, think about you. Please excuse poor letter. English very little, but love very much, just cannot say. I sit by hill at night and my heart hurt for you, but I know cannot be, so I must write and tell you of love. Now feel better. Sayanara Bensan." The letter was signed by Yoshiko and the faint mark of a lip print indicated the sealing with a tender kiss.

Ben read the letter a few more times and then taking his lighter he burnt the letter until only an ash remained. He blew the ash into the night air, then taking the letter from Ruth from his pocket he read about his son's first tooth. He'd be home to see it in just a few more weeks.

Teriko learned of Frank Tucker's death when the boat brought the G.I.s back to the island. She was prepared to lose Frank. She had known that he would be leaving her the next day and she had dreaded the thought of his going into another girl's arms. Now he was her's alone. Her's forever. She took his picture that he had given her and held it to her heart. She loved him so very much and yet she knew that when the ten weeks were up he would be gone. And now he was dead. But she had made him happy, so very happy. "Happier than he had ever been," he had said. And, "she was a nice girl. Such a very nice girl." And now she could hold her head up high because she knew definitely that she was not a "Pig."

At first she cried. For two days she cried and then she went back to work and somehow her whole life was different. Frank Tucker had changed her life and she loved him for it. Love, that was something they had taught each other. Something neither had known and yet once they found it, it made their lives complete.

As soon as Frenchie got through the gate he headed for the souvenir shop that sold boat tickets. They had a lot of literature on travel and Frenchie had already begun planning his itinerary. He would go A.W.O.L. at Camp Drake in Toyko and catch the first train to Mount Fuji. He could climb Fuji and get back to Yokahama the next day. Then a quick tour of Yokahama and a look at the Imperial Palace in Toyko with a fast shopping trip down the Ginza and he'd be ready to make the flight to Washington. What the hell, a couple of days, surely the Army would never miss him. Certainly the President wouldn't have expected him to leave Japan without first climbing Mount Fuji. He was sure he could talk his way out of just a few lost days.

Tom Gomez headed into town with a new attitude toward his mission. He was going to buy some souvenirs for his folks and he was going to do it if he had to crawl on his hands and knees past the Cabarets to that Gift Store. He went past the gate and without looking to his left or right he walked and then ran the last hundred feet. He made it this time and in 15 minutes he had arranged for a big box of gifts to be mailed home. Then again without looking right or left he ran down to the bicycle stand and rented a bicycle. It was late at night when he returned to camp, sober. He purposely missed the party. He figured that drinking just wasn't his cup of tea.

Charlie made a quick trip to the P.X. and then signed out and headed for town. When he arrived at their room, Happy ran to the door and into his waiting arms. "Oh Cholly, I worry so much about you. Someone say you go to Chosen."

"Chosen?" Charlie asked.

"Korea. Japanese say Chosen."

"Well I'll be a...," he said. "We used to call it the Frozen Chosen and I never knew why."

"You go Korea, Cholly?"

"Yeah, we went to Korea, Happy, but now we're back."

"Happy glad you come back Cholly."

Charlie stood at the doorway feeling self-conscious, standing on one leg and then the other. "Happy," he began. "The fellows in our class have all been order Stateside. Real quick like. We're leaving tomorrow."

Tears welled up in Happy's eyes, she bit her lip and held back a sob. "You go Stateside Cholly." Suddenly she looked very helpless and very alone.

"I've got something for you," Charlie said. "I sure hope you like it."

"Never mind present Cholly, what good present if you go away?" She let the tears fall now and she nestled in Charlie's arms and he held her close.

"Well, look at it anyway," Charlie insisted.

He handed it to her and with more persuasion she finally took a look. "It's a ring Chollie. Why you buy me ring when you go Stateside?"

He smiled and held her closer. "Because we're getting married and that is your engagement ring."

She looked baffled. "How we get married Cholly? You say before Chaplain say we no can marry."

"Well, I got it OK'd by a Three Star General, and a Three Star General can fix anything. We're getting married in the Chapel tomorrow morning and you're coming Stateside with me."

"No more, just-for-now wife Cholly?"

"Just forever," he said, pulling her into his arms and kissing her. "Now get yourself dressed up in that new dress I got you from the Sears' Catalog. We're all having a farewell party at the Number One Beer Hall."

When they arrived the party had already started. Boots was up with the band trying hopelessly to show the band how to keep a beat. Sammy was sitting near the door passing out canned goods, cigarettes, chewing gum and piles of yen to everyone. He had really hit it this time. After giving him all the prizes at the Pachinko Parlos, they gave him what Yen they had on hand and then presented him with his very own Pachinko Machine to take Stateside.

Drinks were flowing everywhere and the men were all excitedly making toasts.

"Goodbye Japan," someone shouted.

"To Frank," Ben said and a silence came over the room for a full moment as the men showed their deep respect.

"Goodbye Japan!" someone said, breaking the gloom.

"Goodbye Yokahama!"
"Goodbye Tokyo!"
"Hello Frisco!"
"Hello New Orleans!"
"Goodbye Korea!"
"Goodbye Yoshiko--Goodbye Tomiko."
"HELLO MARIA!" they yelled in unison.

Someone got down on his knees like Al Jolson and sang, "Hello My Mammy."

And so it went on into the night. Wild, happy, excited G.I.s. They were going home. They paraded up and down the streets kissing the girls goodbye. Then they kissed their Australian buddies and if they could have located Captain Thompson and Corporal Tuttle they just might have kissed them too.

THE END

Books by Art Fettig

It Only Hurts When I Frown
Selling Lucky--A Guide to Happiness & Success
How to Hold an Audience in the Hollow of Your Hand
Mentor: Secrets of the Ages
Anatomy of a Speech
16 Great Lucky Selling Ideas
This Is It!
How Funny Are You?--The Humor Game, with Herb True, PhD.
Pos Parenting--A Guide to Greatness
Unfit for Glory

FOR CHILDREN
The Three Robots
Remembering
The Three Robots and the Sandstorm
The Three Robots Find a Grandpa
The Three Robots Discover Their Pos-Abilities
The Pos Activity Book

For a free catalog or information on Art Fettig's services as a professional speaker, contact:

GROWTH UNLIMITED, INC.

Art Fettig, President • 31 East Avenue S • Battle Creek, Michigan 49017
Phone 616-965-2229 or 616-964-4821